THE DAYS WHEN
THE ANIMALS TALKED

THE DAYS
WHEN
THE ANIMALS
TALKED

*Black American Folktales
and How They Came To Be*

WILLIAM J. FAULKNER

ILLUSTRATIONS BY TROY HOWELL

FOLLETT PUBLISHING COMPANY  CHICAGO

ISBN 0–695–40755–4 Titan binding
ISBN 0–695–80755–2 Trade binding

Library of Congress Catalog Card Number: 76–50315
 23456789 / 828180797877

*To my beloved wife,
my inspiration for fifty-seven years, and
to our daughters, Josephine and Marie.*

Contents

A Head Full and a Heart Full of Stories

"PLEASE TELL US A STORY from the book that's inside you!" In varying modes of expression, these beseeching words from the lips of the children and grandchildren of William Faulkner have echoed and reechoed in every age and culture of mankind from the most primitive to the most advanced civilizations. They have been the bridge over which listeners and tellers have crossed from the world of reality into realms of imagination and fantasy. Seeking enchantments that would extend their deepest experiences, eager followers of every age have responded, timelessly, to the demanding call of the ageless art of storytelling.

Drawing upon well remembered, nostalgic scenes from childhood, Dr. Faulkner himself may have made a similar request of his elderly neighbor and friend Simon Brown, in whose home he spent countless hours:

> Simon would sit by the fire in his homemade cane-bottom rocking chair and tell me stories of his life as a slave in Virginia . . . and how hard it was

for our people to live. Or he'd tell me stories out of his imagination or the imagination of others he'd heard around the campfire in the slave quarters years ago. It was a time of great wonder for me. . . ."

Indeed, "it was a time of great wonder"; it was also a time to take a reflective journey into a meaningful past. Wide-eyed and eager, a youthful listener sat in awe as an elderly storyteller unrolled before him a panoramic view into a way of life that was alien to him and yet was a significant part of his heritage. Hearing these tales come alive "under the magic spell of Simon Brown" helped a child to realize that his roots were deep. He gained a clearer understanding of the meaning behind Langston Hughes's words: from the moment Jamestown linked itself with a despicable chain of slavery to the African continent, there was "caught in those chains my hand, NEGRO."

Although physically shackled and inflicted with every cruel, inhuman device that their masters could conceive in an effort to eradicate tribal languages, customs, and beliefs, the first enslaved blacks did not come to these shores empty-handed, nor did they arrive as primitive, soulless clods. Strangers in a new land, they brought an inner strength that could not be broken; they revealed a depth of spirituality that has seldom been matched for its simplicity of expression, its richness in speech and song, its vibrant imagery. Stripped of all physical and psychological armor, these forebears of present-day black Americans persevered under the most adverse conditions.

And fusing their diverse African cultures with those already existing in the Western Hemisphere, they gradually encircled their unsuspecting captors with their creative artistry, venting their emotions in spontaneous oral and musical expressions drawn from the depths of their beings. In the words of the distinguished author Ralph Ellison:

> The history of the American Negro is a most intimate part of American History. Through the very process of slavery came the building of the United States. Negro folklore, evolving within a larger culture which regarded it as inferior, was an especially courageous expression. It announced the Negro's willingness to trust his own experience, his own sensibilities as to the definition of reality, rather than allow his masters to define crucial matters for him. His experience is that of America and the West, and is as rich a body of experience as one would find anywhere. We can view it narrowly as something exotic, folksy, or 'low down' or we may identify ourselves with it and recognize it as an important segment of the larger American experience—not lying at the bottom of it, but intertwined, diffused in its very texture. . . .
>
> (New York: The Viking Press, Inc. Interview with Ralph Ellison from *Writers at Work: The Paris Review Interviews,* Second Series, copyright 1963 by the Paris Review, Inc.)

Confronted with the stress of living through one of the most sordid periods of our nation's history, slaves found mental and emotional escape from the debilitating effects of their confinement in the folktales told by skilled raconteurs such as Simon Brown. These storytellers gave to their listeners, lacking in worldly knowledge and limited in learning, narratives that contained elements of realism and magic in situations and characters with which they were familiar. They infused their tellings with dramatic power. This attribute appealed to the emotions; it satisfied inner cravings, cloaked signs of unrest, evoked laughter, provided solace, and fostered a temporary release from the misery of a chaotic existence.

Possessing a wide repertoire of tales, a storyteller could draw forth oral retellings based upon personal, real-life situations. Here, the urge to share something of the heart and the spirit would prompt a teller to recreate what had been seen or experienced. Thus, in the role of a recorder, he would relate to his listeners news of an event that may have had a significant effect upon his own or their own lives, as in the tales "A Slave's Dangerous Courtship" and "Simon and the Pater-rollers." Further, as an interpreter, a storyteller would give the account both depth and fullness by supplying needed embellishments of detail and color.

As an oral artist, a teller would be put to the supreme test when it became necessary to fashion a tale in a language and style that harmonized, perfectly, with the culture and spirit of the people from which the story had come. Although cultures share many universal traits, each group of people fashions its own cultural identity in the evolution of the creative process by extracting needed elements from the varying factors of traditions and social and economic conditions. Simon Brown had mastered this artistry:

> He had been sustained by the soul force of his people's tales, and being a storyteller himself, he could share that sustenance with his fellows. . . . He was an artist who took his audience into his own special world of woods and fields, where they visited his friends, the birds and beasts, and learned the secrets of how they lived. And while they learned how these fantastical creatures lived, they often learned how they, too, should live.

The early black storytellers supplemented these personal accounts with the more traditional types of folktales that have now become integral parts of the foundation of American folklore. Their rich mosaic of oral literature included a wide array of animal, haunt, and preacher stories, conjure tales, master/slave anecdotes, exaggerations or lying tales, trickster yarns, homilies and proverbs, riddles, ballads, epics, hero tales and legends, games, sermons, blues, spirituals, slave and work songs. Handed down in the oral tradition from generation to generation, this proliferation of stories mirrored the diverse cultural and value systems found in numerous disparate Negro communities.

Representative of this wealth of black folklore was the

genre animal tales, from which Simon Brown recreated many of his stories. Against a backdrop of plantation lands, riverbanks, crops, fields, deep woods, caves, country roads, and other familiar locales, the animal characters acted out their roles. Parading through almost all of these popular narratives was Brer Rabbit, who was adopted by American Negro slaves as their culture hero.

> . . . through Brer Rabbit and the tales of his daring, enslaved blacks were able to see themselves not only as morally superior to their white masters, but as ultimately triumphant over them.

Although physically small and weak, Brer Rabbit was the proud owner of other significant qualities. A skilled trickster and devilish practical joker, he was also an accomplished lady's man; such tales as "Brer Wolf's Magic Gate," "Brer Rabbit Keeps His Word," and "Brer Rabbit Goes a-Courting" clearly reveal these talents. But it was his rare and remarkable wit, which enabled him to extricate himself from difficulties, that particularly pleased those who listened to such tales as "Brer Bear Gets a Taste of Man" and "Brer Fox Meets Mister Trouble."

The perceptive storytellers of slavery days thus exploited the naiveté of their supposedly intellectually superior white masters, who duped themselves into falsely believing that these stories merely served as harmless products of a "childlike" people to amuse illiterate listeners or to entertain the master's children. The oral artists excelled in the art of projecting protests, personal experiences, hopes, and defeats in the subtle guise of simplistic fictional narratives. Indeed, as cogently expressed by the noted folklorist Harold Courlander in his excellent collection *A Treasury of Afro-American Folklore* (New York: Crown Publishers, Inc., 1976):

> . . . black oral literature in the United States . . . is an oral literature with a special personality, often containing implicit or explicit intellectual or emotional responses to the injustices and inequities inherent in the historic relationship of blacks to the mainstream culture. It contains elements of humor, irony, criticism and poetry that, in a literary sense, are uniquely expressed. It observes, it comments, it narrates. It ranges from humorous nonsense to profound and moving reflections of the human experience. . . .the roots of the literature are in the open fields of the Southland, the sharecropped farms, the plantations of slavery and postslavery times, the small southern towns, and the little churches that were a focus of social contact as well as a vital source of emotional enrichment. As we read it today, this oral literature not only tells us much about the past, but also a great deal about the present.

The need is great to perfect the art of storytelling, to keep alive this fund of stories that forms a body of learning of black culture and a tradition that is, truly, American. It is imperative to pass these gifts on as parts of a living heritage to those who are yet to come, for these will be the armor with which a seeker after truth may find roots, beauty, and a meaning to life. Recognizing this challenge in a tangible manner with this collection of Negro lore, Dr. Faulkner responds to the age-old request, "Please tell us a story from the book that's inside you."

SPENCER G. SHAW
Professor of Librarianship
University of Washington
Seattle, Washington

FOREWORD

Sparks of Art—
Shared and Reshared

SPARKS OF ART as brilliant as those raining from the hearth on which a hickory log was placed came from former slave Simon Brown as he recounted tales of slavery to William John Faulkner. "It was," Reverend Faulkner remarks, "in the time of my imagination—when it was developing rapidly and my curiosity to know was like an obsession." Spiritual as well as artistic bonds were established as Simon became young Faulkner's friend—mentor—hero.

That association, begun in 1900 when Faulkner was only ten and lasting for seven years, has since resulted in the appearance of one of the most important collections of Afro-American folktales ever assembled. Not only do we find in *The Days When the Animals Talked* a rich yield of never-before-published Brer Rabbit stories and revealing tales of slave life, but we meet an artist of unmistakable genius, for surely Simon Brown emerges from these pages fully worthy of that title.

Reverend Faulkner's treatment of the narratives makes it evident that Simon, who helped to keep alive the folk tradition by recounting tales in unforgettable fashion, was an artist capable of virtually singing his stories. Simon's re-creation of the events, personalities, and atmosphere of thirty years of slavery is thus an invaluable resource for those who would understand slavery and its consequences in our lives today.

In the entire body of folk literature of Afro-Americans, it is hard to find tales as important for what they tell us about slave life as "How the Slaves Helped Each Other" and as remarkable for sheer artistic expression as "The Tiger and the Big Wind." In "How the Slaves Helped Each Other," as dance grows out of rejoicing, sermon rises to song, and hope triumphs over sorrow, more is revealed about slave culture than in whole books on slavery by "experts." "The Tiger and the Big Wind," while conveying a deep spiritual truth, stands as a supreme expression of the folktale as art. It reads very well on paper, but for full effect should be read aloud.

When a great storyteller like Reverend Faulkner uses the rhythms and sounds of humans to make the animals talk in ways peculiarly their own yet ours, a whole new world of reality comes alive in our ears. And now, with the appearance of this book, Reverend Faulkner's gifts as a storyteller, modeled after those of Simon Brown himself, have been matched by his undoubted importance as a collector of tales of black America.

STERLING STUCKEY
Associate Professor of History
Northwestern University
Evanston, Illinois

Introduction

AN OLD MAN NAMED SIMON BROWN began telling me
exciting animal and ghost stories when I was about ten
years old. Simon had been a slave in Virginia, but in his
later years, as a freedman, he helped my widowed mother
work our tiny farm near the village of Society Hill,
South Carolina. As a boy, I loved to carry lunch to Simon
in the field or to visit him in the evening in the "downstairs house," the small house adjacent to my family's
home. I loved to see Simon because that meant I could
hear him—hear him tell, with his rich voice and rousing
gestures, the fascinating tales my black ancestors had
told in slavery times.

As a child, I responded to the stories simply as stories,
lively tales about animals who walked and talked and
lived together in harmony or discord much as people did.
But as I grew older, I realized the stories were not just
children's entertainments, but were deeply significant al-
legories created by a tortured, subjugated people to sustain and encourage themselves in a hostile world. And,
taken together, the seemingly simple stories—the folk-

tales of black Americans—formed a subtle but powerful body of protest literature.

Hundreds of thousands of Africans died in the squalid holds of slave ships crossing the Atlantic, or committed suicide by jumping overboard, or were killed by the breaking-in whippings of their overlords. Those who survived met the powerful armed force of the American slave system with a matching degree of soul force, which enabled them not only to live but to grow strong and multiply. This soul force found voice in many of the slaves' religious songs and folktales; there, tucked among innocent-sounding praises to God and descriptions of antic animals, were veiled protests against slavery and a deep-seated faith that all slaves would one day be free.

While the slave system tried to destroy him, the Afro-American kept his spirit alive and hopeful through his faith in a God of love and justice and through his imagination, which allowed him to escape his destitute reality. Whether working or resting, whether in joy or in suffering, he managed to pray and sing and tell folktales. Many times, in the field, black voices would sing, "Over my head, there's music in the air; There must be a God somewhere." And many times white ears would hear only the slaves' longing to go to Heaven when, in fact, the words carried a hidden message of plans for a slave's liberation.

Slaves often felt that they lived closer to God than their masters because they could "talk with God" and were therefore better human beings. A legend illustrates this belief:

Once a crew of slaves had worked to exhaustion in a hot cotton field, while their owner sat comfortably on his piazza drinking a julep. When the slaves declared they could work no more, their leader said, "John the Conqueror wouldn't like that. He told me to tell you not to give up now. If you do, you'll all get a beating and be given a bigger task to do. Instead, he said to reach inside your hearts and bring out a song, a song of salvation, of freedom. You've got a lot of songs of salvation in your hearts." With that, the slaves began to sing, and they were refreshed. Then their leader looked toward their master and said, "In a way, I feel sorry for that white man, because he's not on speaking terms with God. He's a lost soul."

Religious faith indeed strengthened the black people's will to survive—and to triumph.

So did their folktales. The Afro-American slaves had no weapons against their oppressors. So, like their forebears in Africa, they used their folklore to comment on good and evil in their lives, depending on the cloak of fiction to protect themselves and their families from retribution. Many of the animal stories of black Americans were clever denunciations of the brutal slave system or warnings against the evil designs of white society. Simon Brown's story of "How the Cow Went Under the Ground" is a good example of subtle warning. In it, Brer Rabbit, though no match in size and strength for Brer Bear, uses wit and cunning to replace his stolen cow and make a laughingstock of Brer Bear. While one moral seems apparent, the true moral is not openly revealed by the storyteller; it lies hidden between the lines for his soul brothers and sisters to see and understand.

It is not surprising that the slaves adopted the rabbit as their hero and called it brother, or "brer." Like themselves, an overpowered minority, the rabbit was small and almost defenseless physically. It depended on its cleverness and constant vigilance for survival. As Simon Brown once said, "Brer Rabbit can't fight like a wildcat or climb a tree. But he's got big eyes that can see to the front and the sides and behind without turning his head. He's got long legs and a heap o' sense! To the slave, he's like a brother!"

The slaves also perceived the rabbit as being, like themselves, an innocent victim pursued by larger, more powerful enemies. Brer Rabbit was virtuous, on the side of God. His antagonists were wicked, on the side of the Devil. As the slaves identified with the rabbit, they felt themselves to be allied with God, and their white adversaries to be henchmen of the Devil.

Thus, through Brer Rabbit and the tales of his daring, enslaved blacks were able to see themselves not only as morally superior to their white masters, but as ultimately triumphant over them. Of course, they dared not reveal this vision to their oppressors. They could only cherish the courage and self-respect it gave them and thank God for its comfort.

Now, Simon Brown was one such slave. He had been sustained by the soul force of his people's tales, and being a storyteller himself, he could share that sustenance with his fellows. He could imitate the voices of the animals, make them "talk like menfolks," and dramatize their actions. He could frighten eager listeners when he roared like Brer Tiger or make them laugh when he squeaked like Brer Rabbit. In fact, all nature seemed to come alive under the magic spell of Simon Brown. He was an artist who took his audience into his own special world of woods and fields, where they visited his friends, the birds and beasts, and learned the secrets of how they lived. And while they learned how these fantastical creatures lived, they often learned how they, too, should live.

Simon Brown's folktales so deeply impressed me that, although more than seventy years have passed since I first heard them, I have forgotten only a few. In their original form, the tales were told in dialect, or broken English. This language of the slaves was largely a combination of African words and cockney English as it was spoken by the European overseers. This was particularly true in coastal South Carolina. The Gullah dialect, which Simon Brown spoke and which is still spoken on the off-coast islands, contains many purely African words: *keely hawk* for *sparrow hawk, cooter* for *turtle, tote* for *carry, pinder* for *peanut, enty* for *isn't it,* and *yunner* for *you-all. Brer,* a contraction of *brother,* also appears as *br'r, brudder,* and *bubbah. Sis* is often used instead of *sister.*

In retelling Simon Brown's stories, I have retained some dialectal words, but have largely used standard English. Although I feel that something is lost in the translation, I am opposed to allowing children, black or white, to use dialectal speech in school, and I would not want this book to encourage such language patterns.

The heavy use of dialect has given black folktales and their tellers an Uncle Remus image. The idea of black folk literature as simply funny stories told by an engaging but ignorant and obsequious old black man still dominates the thinking of white Americans, and has caused many sensitive black Americans to reject an invaluable heritage. In accepting this sorry image, in failing to perceive the symbolism and significance underlying the stories, both blacks and whites have suffered an incalculable loss.

I have two hopes in retelling these tales. The first is to place the folktales of Simon Brown and other black storytellers in their proper perspective in the black people's centuries-old struggle against injustice and exploitation. The second is to establish these storytellers as intelligent and gifted artists whose creations are worthy of honor among the folk literatures of the world.

PART I
THE SETTING

Black Slave Tales

A Slave's
Dangerous Courtship

I WAS A FREQUENT VISITOR of Simon Brown's during the years he lived in the "downstairs house" next to my family's home. In the center of Simon's house stood a huge brick chimney with two wide fireplaces, one on either side. Simon liked to spend his evenings there, in the warmth and glow of the fire. He'd sit in his home-made cane-bottom rocking chair and tell me stories of his life as a slave in Virginia—the Old Dominion State, he called it—and how hard it was for our people to live. Or he'd tell me stories out of his imagination or the imagination of others he'd heard around the campfire in the slave quarters years ago. It was a time of great wonder for me.

One evening Simon sat rocking slowly in his chair in front of his fireplace. The three-foot oak logs had been burning for several hours, and the room was warm and shadowy. Red-hot coals glowed under the logs in the center, while feathery white ashes covered the hearth from one end to the other. All was so quiet and ghost-like when I entered that I thought the old man was asleep. But he turned his head toward me and smiled a welcome.

Without saying a word, he motioned for me to sit near him, on a small hickory stool with a black-and-white cowhide bottom. Then he reached in his pocket, fished out his worn clay pipe with the bamboo stem, and cut small chips of Old Mule plug tobacco into the bowl. When the bowl was full, he raked a burning coal from the hearth with a poker, picked it up with his horny fingers, and quickly pressed it into the pipe. He puffed and puffed until the smoke came out of his mouth, while I sat shocked at seeing a man handle a coal of fire without being burned.

Then Simon spoke quietly.

I was just looking into the fire, Willie, and thinking away back into my slave days when I was a young courting-man. I was handsome, if I do say so myself, and I cut quite a figure with the pretty girls who worked in my master's Big House. I was a house-servant in those days myself—butler to Master John Brown. Old Master liked me, and one Christmas he gave me a pair of fine patent leather boots.

Now, the prettiest girl in the county lived two plantations away from us. She was the cook for the McCrackens. Ellen was her name. She was as brown as a chestnut and had long, straight black hair that reached to her waist. I loved her so much that I asked Master John if I could marry her.

He answered, "Yes, Simon, if she'll have you. I'll make

arrangements to buy her from Mister McCracken, so that you two can live here on my place."

"Thank you, sir," I said. "Could I have a pass for next Sunday to go over there and speak for her hand?"

The master said the pass would be ready.

In those days in Virginia, slaves didn't have much of a wedding. Most times they couldn't even have a preacher. The master would stand before the black couple and say something like this:

"Jim, do you love Sally?"

"Yes, sir," Jim would respond.

"Sally, do you love Jim?"

"Yes, sir," she would reply.

"Then I pronounce you man and wife," the master would say.

And that was all, except that some masters would make the couple jump over a broomstick before they'd say they were married. The slaves didn't like this, because it made the white people laugh. But they couldn't do anything about it if their masters were mean. My master had promised me that his own preacher would marry Ellen and me.

So the next Sunday, with my pass in my pocket, I went over to the McCrackens' place to see Ellen. And I wore my shiny new boots. She was cooking supper in the kitchen, which was a house out in the yard behind the Big House. She was glad to see me and invited me to come in. I sat on a windowsill, with my feet hanging down inside the kitchen and my face toward a window in the opposite wall. Just as I was about to ask Ellen if she would marry me, I saw young Jim McCracken, the master's son, coming toward the open window with a shotgun in his hand.

Jim cursed me and shouted, "Simon, I told you once before to stay off my daddy's place and leave Ellen alone. She's my gal, and nobody else will ever have her. She's too good-looking for any black man, slave or free. So get going before I blow your head off!" With that, Jim raised the gun to his shoulder and aimed at my head.

Before he could pull the trigger, I fell backward in a somersault and landed on my feet. "Bam!" went the gun, but the shots missed me. Out over the field I raced. Jim dropped his gun and started out to catch me. He even called for his brother Ben to help him. By that time, I was away out in the plowed field, ahead of both brothers. I stopped long enough to take off my boots and get a fresh start..Now, I knew those two soft buckra (aristocratic whites) would never catch me in a footrace. Pretty soon I lost sight of them, and I got home safe and sound. But I was mad as a hornet—to think that a slave man couldn't even court a slave woman because a white man wanted her for his concubine.

Now, Jim and Ben McCracken vowed that if ever I came on their plantation again, they'd whip me to death or otherwise kill me. I knew my life was in danger every time I went to see Ellen, but I wasn't easily discouraged. I was the fastest runner, the strongest wrestler, and the best boxer in the county, and in a fair fight I wasn't afraid of any man who walked, black or white. So I went on courting Ellen.

One day, though, as I was leaving Ellen's place late in the afternoon by a secret footpath, both of the McCrackens rushed out of hiding and jumped me. The older one, Ben, grabbed me from behind and held me around the waist, while Jim attacked from the front with a hunting knife. I tried to break Ben's hold, but couldn't. As Jim came at me with the knife, I knocked him to the ground with my fists and kicked him in the head. Then I tried to break Ben's grip by butting him with the back of my head. But Ben held on and hollered to his brother, "Get up from there and bring your knife around here to his back. Jab him in the neck and shoulder. That'll get him."

For a time, I was able to turn myself and Ben around every time Jim came at my back. And by kicking and fighting with my fists, I kept him beyond cutting distance. Finally, though, Jim rushed in from behind, reached over Ben, and drove that knife blade deep in my shoulder. I yelped in pain, then broke loose and ran into a field of tall corn. Those McCrackens were so sure I'd die, they didn't even try to follow.

But, Willie, I kept on traveling through that cornfield, bleeding so bad I had to hold on to the cornstalks to stay up. I was scared to lie down for fear I'd never get up again. But I was growing weaker and weaker. I must have broken a road through that cornfield six-foot wide. I kept praying to the Lord to help me find a drink of water, or I'd surely die. Then, right before me, was a ditch bank. I turned the stalks loose and grabbed the bushes and half rolled down into the ditch. But—Lord have mercy—the only water there was in mud puddles.

Never mind, I was so thirsty from loss of blood that I just lay down in one of those puddles and drank that muddy water—wiggle-tails, tadpoles, and all. Then I rested a bit, until I could tear off a piece of my shirt to stuff in the wound in my shoulder and stop the bleeding.

By and by, I was able to pull myself up the other side of the ditch. I saw a widow woman's house over by the road. She was a white woman—and a good Christian lady. If I could just manage to drag myself to her yard, I knew she'd help me. Well, I managed, and when she saw me, she almost fainted. I was bloody and muddy from head to foot, and almost dead.

The good lady screamed, "What on earth's the matter with you, Simon?"

"The McCracken boys stabbed me, Miss Jessie," I moaned. "Please, ma'am, get word to Master John Brown to send the wagon for me quick as he can—else I'm going to die."

Miss Jessie called a manservant to put me on a pile of cotton on her piazza, then sent him scurrying to my master's place for help. I must have fainted dead away then, because I didn't know anything more until I came to the next day in my own little cabin. And I guess the good Lord didn't want me yet, for with careful nursing, I grew strong again and lived to face those McCracken brothers another day.

When Simon's story was over, he pulled off his shirt, turned his back to the blazing hearth, and showed me the wound on his left shoulder where Jim McCracken had stabbed him. I felt the scar with my fingers and believed every word he had told me.

"But, Willie," he said proudly, "remember, that's the only wound on my back. I carry no stripes across my back, because I never let any man whip me. He would have had to kill me first. And even then, I would have carried him down with me. No, sir, Simon Brown was never whipped. I was a mighty man in those days."

Simon Marries Ellen

A FEW NIGHTS EARLIER, when I had visited Simon Brown, he had told me how close he'd come to death the time Ben and Jim McCracken stabbed him on his way home from courting Ellen. He had lain sick abed for several days after the attack. "But," he'd said, "my constitution was so strong it must have been made of iron," and in a few weeks, he was as good as new.

This evening, as I sat with Simon, I asked if he and Ellen were ever married. The old man closed his eyes as if he were in a deep study, and his voice seemed far away when he answered.

Yes, Willie, Ellen and me, we got married. But we had a heap of trouble before it came off. You see, in slavery days, black people weren't treated like human beings, but like work animals. It happened all over the South that masters or the sons of masters picked out the good-looking slave girls for themselves. They kept them for their common-law wives and had children by them. Many plantation owners had two families—one white and one black—all living in the same yard. The white family lived in the Big House, and the black family lived in a cabin. A slave man might be deep in love with a slave girl, the way I was with Ellen, but he dared not keep company with her if her master objected.

What made me despise the McCracken boys so much was they were such low-down creatures. Like many white men all over the South, they appeared to me—and to all the slaves mostly—to be lower than the beasts of the woods. We had no real respect for them. A wolf or a tiger would fight to defend his young. He would never forsake his children. But a white man would force a slave woman to have children by him and then hold his own blood offspring in slavery. For money, he'd make them work for him for nothing and even take them away from their mother and sell them off like hogs or cattle at market. That's about as wicked and dirty as a man can be.

And, yet, we slaves were taught that the master was a Christian and that every white man was better than a black man, slave or free. We grinned in his face and said, "Yes, sir, that's so, Master," but behind his back we cursed him. So it was with me and the McCracken boys. In my heart, I felt I was a better man than they were and by and by I would outdo them and take Ellen from them.

In fact, I felt that both Ellen and I, by blood, should have been born free. Her father and mine were both buckra—so-called "quality" white folks—and our mothers were slaves. Our skins weren't black or white, but brown. And we were real, sure-enough half-brother and half-sister to all our fathers' pure-white children. Everybody around knew we were blood kin to buckra, but that made no difference—we were slaves all the same. But deep down inside us slaves, hidden from the white men, our self-respect was always there. But, like Brer Rabbit, we had to be deceitful and use our heads to stay alive.

Still, there were times a slave just had to come out in the open and stand up like a man against his white enemy. And that's what I had to do with those McCracken boys.

So, when I got good and strong, I went to Master John Brown and told him again that I wanted to marry Ellen, Master McCracken's cook. I told him how young Master Ben and Master Jim had ordered me off their daddy's place and had almost cut me to death when I went back to court Ellen. I told Master John how I was determined to marry her no matter what happened, and I asked him please to try to buy Ellen and bring her to our place where we could live together as man and wife. I swore that he and old Missy, his wife, would love Ellen's good cooking.

"Simon," said Master John, "I'll do it for you." And so he bought Ellen from Master McCracken for fifteen hundred dollars cash. That was a steep price for a woman slave. But she was worth every cent of it.

The next Sunday afternoon Ellen and I were united in marriage by Master John Brown's own preacher, just as if we were human beings—in fact, almost as if we were members of Master John's own family. We stood under a wide chinaberry tree in the front yard. Old Master and

Missy and all their children, and the house-servants too, sat on the front piazza. And the field hands came up from the slave quarters and stood around the yard as witnesses.

After the words were said, everybody celebrated the wedding at a big barbecue in the backyard. The day before, Master John had ordered that three pigs be killed and dressed, and pits be dug for their cooking. All through the night men and women had kept the hickory sticks and chips burning in the pits for the roasting of the pigs. They'd basted the hams and shoulders and ribs with a special hot-spiced sauce, and every so often they'd turned the pieces of meat over, to be evenly browned. At another pit of coals, a whole pig was being roasted on a spit with a handle for turning. This pig, too, was covered with hot sauce, brushed on by a sort of long-handled cloth mop dipped in a lard can full of sauce.

All day Sunday the sweet, tangy smell of the barbecue drifted over the plantation, so by the time of the wedding, everybody's mouth was watering. Hot corn bread was cooking in wide pans, too. And gallons and gallons of sweetened water, made from sugarcane syrup and cool water, were standing in the shade to wash the feast down.

My wedding was the biggest and happiest for miles around. And Ellen was the proudest bride you could find. Little did I know that big trouble from the McCracken boys was soon to catch up with me again. But I'll tell you about that later, Willie. I'm tired and sleepy now. Good night.

Simon Challenges the McCrackens

SEVERAL NIGHTS LATER, I quietly stole into Simon's room with the huge fireplace. As usual, he was half-dozing before the warm fire. In his hand he held a long hickory stick, which he used as a poker. As I sat on the leather-bottomed stool, he stirred the ashes with his stick and pulled out a couple of small sweet potatoes—slips, he called them. They were the kind he planted in early spring in my mother's hotbed. The sprouts would be set out in rows later in her potato patch. When the crop was gathered in the fall, Simon would bank, or bury, the big potatoes in large dirt-covered mounds, safe from the frost. The little ones, the slips, he would cover in a smaller bank.

"Here, Willie," he said. "Help yourself to these potato slips while they're hot."

I blew off the ashes and ate the potatoes, peelings and all. They were delicious.

"Brother Simon," I asked, "please tell me what happened with the McCracken boys after your master bought Ellen from their father, and you and Ellen were married."

The old man looked into the fire for a long time. Then he said, "Willie, that's been a long, long time ago, but I remember it as clear as if it was yesterday." He smiled, leaned back in his rocker, and started to talk.

In the wintertime on the plantations, the slaves couldn't do much work in the fields. So the master would set tasks for them to do in the barns or the lots or on the fences and such. On cold days, the men would butcher hogs, and the women would help make sausage and headcheese. But on rainy days, we would mostly shuck corn.

Now, on this one rainy day, I was in the barn helping with the corn shucking. Everybody was singing and having a good time. But every time I went between the barn and the Big House, I kept on the lookout for those two scoundrels—those McCracken boys—to jump me. Ever since they'd lost Ellen, they'd sent messages that my days were numbered, that they were coming over to Master John's place one day and beat me to death before he could save me. You see, in those days, if a white man killed a slave, the court wouldn't try him for murder, but would only make him pay the slave's master for the loss of a servant or field hand.

So, during the corn shucking, I made preparations to defend myself if the McCrackens came. The rain had let up a short spell, and pretty soon I heard horses coming. Up rode Ben and Jim. They jumped off their horses and headed for the barn. Each man held a bullwhip—the kind generally used for punishing slaves. The only difference now was that the McCrackens had tied a ten-penny nail in the end of each whip. This was meant to burst the hide of any man it struck.

I saw from the barn door that those devils really meant to kill me. Everybody in the barn stopped singing, they were so scared. Master John Brown didn't see the McCrackens, because the barn was about fifty yards behind the Big House, and nobody could get out to call him. I was caught like a pig in a pen.

Ben and Jim started toward the open barn door, whips coiled in their hands. Their faces were mean and cruel as tigers'. Then one of them called out, "Simon Brown, come forth!" I didn't move. "Come forth, Simon, and take your lashing like a dog, or we'll come in there and drag you out by your heels. Come forth, Simon Brown!"

I reached down under a pile of corn shucks and felt for a six-pronged pitchfork I had hidden there. When I found it, I stood up and walked to the door. There I stood for a minute, the fork in my hands, looking both of those cowards straight in the eye. Then I jumped out into the yard and roared like a panther, "Simon's a-coming! And he's ready to die!" I started marching on those two low buckra, pointing the pitchfork straight at their hearts and yelling, "One of you is going to die, maybe both of you, if you dare to raise a whip hand!"

Their faces turned as white as chalk, and before I could get within stabbing distance, they both turned tail and fled. They jumped on their horses and cantered away down the road toward home. And that was the last time I ever had any trouble with the McCracken boys.

No, sir, as I told you before, I never was thrashed in all my slave days, and everybody around knew I never intended to be. And no white man ever bothered Ellen after that.

Simon held his head high and thumped the rocker arm with his fist a time or two, feeling his pride. Then his face broke into a grin, and he went on with a chuckle.

No, no white man ever bothered Ellen again—but a white *woman* bothered *me*. As I told you before, Willie, I was a handsome young fellow in my day. So I had to watch out lest I got into trouble with the womenfolk on the plantation—both black and white.

One day, when I was a butler in Master John Brown's house, one of his daughters sent word to Ellen, who was

the cook, that she was sick and I should fetch her breakfast up to her room. I took a silver tray with the lady's
breakfast upstairs and knocked on her door. And she
said, "Come in." When I went inside, she was still in
bed, with only her lace nightgown on. She ordered me to
shut the door, then said, "Simon, lock that door and give
me the key."

All of a sudden I froze and stood there scared stiff.
Then, quick as lightning, my "blind god" said to me,
"Man, drop those dishes and run." And that's just what
I did. I flew out of that room and down the stairs to the
kitchen, and I told Ellen what had happened.

"Cool off, Simon," she said. "Nothing's going to happen to you. I'll just tell the maid to go up and clean the
mess. But if I were you, I'd ask Master John to change
you from a butler to a yardman. You'll be safer looking
after the livestock in the barnyard than after the womenfolk here in the Big House."

I spoke to Master that same day, and he made me
headman over the horses and mules and such and put
me in charge of the smokehouse. Ellen and I both
breathed easier after that.

Fishing with Bare Hands

ALWAYS EAGER TO HEAR his many stories and true-life adventures, I followed Simon Brown around at every opportunity. If Simon was out working on my family's farm, which was three miles from our house, and my mother wanted me to take our milk cow, Betsy, to graze in the farm pasture, I never balked at the hike. I'd do anything to be with Simon.

One day, when I took Betsy out to graze, I met Simon in the pasture, eating lunch under a chinaberry tree alongside Spot Mill Creek. I flopped on the grass at his side, looked up at him hopefully, and waited. He didn't disappoint me. Smiling and nodding toward the creek, he began his story.

When I was a slave boy, we didn't have any hooks and lines to fish with, the way you do today, Willie. We used to go fishing with our bare hands and crocus sacks.

Sometimes in the summer when the river would get low, water would be left only in hollow places or low places in the riverbed, and that water would be muddy and not running at all. Then the other boys and I would go in there and stir that water around with sticks and with our feet. That made the catfish move around, and we grabbed them with both hands. While one boy held open the sack, the others dumped the fish inside.

But sometimes, when we reached into a muddy hole, we found a water moccasin in there, too. One day I ran my hand into a hollow in the riverbank, and when I pulled it out, I had a snake. Man, I threw him halfway across the riverbed before he could bite me. Yes, sir, that was exciting fishing. I'll tell you that right now.

Sometimes hard times came, and terrible droughts hit the land. Then the ponds and riverbeds dried up completely. I remember a pond close by us where in good weather you could always find half a dozen loggerhead cooters—that is, turtles—sitting on a log out in the middle. When you got close to them, they jumped off the log into the water, and you couldn't find them anyplace. But when droughts came, that old pond just clean dried up. There was no water to be seen from one side of the bank to the other. And there were no turtles to be seen, either. So the people had to go hungry, without meat.

But you know, the Lord is good. He put those turtles in that pond, and every year when the rains came and the pond filled up again, those same turtles came back. So we boys figured those turtles must stay in the bottom of that pond, even when the water dried up. And we set out to find them.

We walked out across the bottom of that pond, and it was so dry and hard our feet didn't sink in the mud at all. Then I remembered what some old folks used to say: "If you find a kind of saucer in the bottom of a pond, there's a turtle down there." So we went home and cut some sharp sticks and drove a tenpenny nail in the end of each one. I fetched a shovel, and we came back to the pond, ready to "sound" for those turtles.

Yes, Willie, we were going to find those turtles by sounding. When we spotted the first saucer, or low place, in the pond, we took one of our sharp sticks and poked it down into the ground. When the nail hit something hard like a rock, we knew that was the back of a turtle. So we dug in that spot, and sure enough there was a great big loggerhead turtle right down about two feet below the top of the ground. And you know, he had kind of a loblolly down there—a hole two feet underground with water in it—and he was living in that water. Yes, sir, that old cooter had made a place down there where he could live until the pond filled up again.

Well, we sounded all over that pond, and the first day we dug out from under the ground thirteen turtles. Some of them were so big they covered the bottom of a washtub. Now we had plenty of meat to eat, for our own families and for other people on the plantation. And you can be sure we had plenty of pride in ourselves, too.

Simon and the Pater-rollers

IN ALMOST EVERY COMMUNITY in the South, tales could be told about the cruelty and brutality of the night riders whom the slaves called pater-rollers. Under the law, pater-rollers were not allowed to kill a slave, because he was valuable property to his owner. However, they could whip a slave for the least offense. The tyranny of the pater-rollers added to the agony of enslaved blacks and made the thwarting of these self-proclaimed judges a grim pleasure.

Like every ex-slave, Simon Brown had feared and hated the pater-rollers and had stored up tales about them. These are some of the happier ones.

When I was a little boy, the slaves used to hold prayer meetings in a cabin out in the middle of a field. A road ran by the cabin, so the pater-rollers could ride right up on their horses.

Now, the pater-rollers were official highwaymen who rode around catching runaway slaves and examining slaves to see if they had passes if they were off their own plantations. They also checked on prayer meetings and other gatherings to hear what the slaves were talking about. So, during the meeting, while the grown-ups were singing and praying in the cabin, I was put out on the front steps as a watch boy to tell the people inside when the pater-rollers were coming.

While I watched down the road, I listened to what went on inside. The preacher was praying to the Lord something like this: "Oh, Lord, look down in pity on us poor slaves. Please, Lord, the load of slavery is so heavy it's about to destroy us all. The grass in the cotton field is so high. The sun is so hot. We almost perish in the middle of the day. Do, Master, have mercy and help us please." And the folks inside shouted, "Yes, Lord," and "Amen," and carried on.

Then I heard the pater-rollers on their horses cantering up the road, coming to the meeting house. Quickly I cracked the door and hollered inside, "Pater-rollers are coming! Pater-rollers are coming!" And when those white men rode up in the yard, they listened to what the slave preacher was saying. By then the preacher had changed his prayer and was saying, "Please, Jesus, help us poor creatures to be faithful to old Master and old Missy. Enable us to do the task in the field tomorrow that they set for us. Help us to be faithful servants and obey our masters. Please, Sir, hear our prayer."

When those pater-rollers heard that, they said, "Everything's all right in there," and they jumped on their horses and galloped away down the road. Then I cracked the door again and yelled, "The pater-rollers are gone. The pater-rollers are gone."

The preacher-man smiled and lifted his arms and said, "Do, Jesus, forgive us for those lies we just prayed, for You know how hard we suffer down here and how we pray for freedom." And then all the people went back to singing and praying for deliverance from their troubles.

When I was older and allowed to go to parties on neighboring plantations, I had lots of run-ins with the pater-rollers. Whenever there was a slave party going on, the pater-rollers would ride up and demand to see the passes of everybody there. If they found a man or even a woman without a pass, they might grab the slave, drag him out into the yard, and hold him across a barrel with his head down while they whipped him as long as they pleased. And nobody dared to interfere.

Well, I got tired of all that meanness and made a plot to get even with the pater-rollers. So at the next party, we built a big fire in the fireplace and threw the embers into one corner and covered them with ashes. This made the ashes very hot. Some time later, while the quilting party was in full swing, a knock came on the door. Somebody whispered, "It's the pater-rollers!"

"You-all just stand back, please," I said. Then another man and I picked up two big shovels we'd brought into the cabin earlier, filled them with red-hot coals and ashes, and ran over to the door.

By that time, the pater-rollers were pounding on the door and hollering, "Come on out. Come on out."

I shouted back, "Fling open that door. Fling open that door."

And when someone flung open that door, we just took those hot ashes and coals and threw them right into the faces and down the chests of those old pater-rollers. Oh, boy, did they scratch and scramble trying to get that heat off! And while they were busy, all of us fellows escaped, so the varmints didn't catch us that night.

Another night, at a candy pulling that I and some friends went to without passes, we decided to play another kind of trick on the pater-rollers. They came while the music and fun was going on inside the cabin, but this time they stayed on their horses and hollered from the yard, "Come on out. Come on out. We're going to get you!"

Then, before you could blink an eye, a bunch of us slaves ran out of the cabin and between the horses. Down the big road we went, with the pater-rollers right behind us. Then we cut to the left down a wagon road through the woods, and down that same road through the woods came the pater-rollers, riding hard. But all of a sudden something snatched every one of those villains off his horse, and they all went whirling through the air while the horses raced on without them. By the time the pater-rollers hit the ground, all of us slaves were gone, and with the breath knocked out of them, they didn't catch a single one of us that night, either.

You know, Willie, a black grapevine is a mighty strong

vine. You can't break it. Folks make ropes and swings out of it. Well, we'd stretched a grapevine across that road just high enough to catch a man but miss a horse's head. And I'm telling you, that vine sure did mess those pater-rollers up that night.

How the Slaves Helped Each Other

A FEW DAYS AFTER he had told me about the pater-rollers' visit to the prayer meeting, Simon Brown said, "Yes, Willie, we slaves had to make our own way in this old world. We didn't have any church in those days, and we didn't have any hospital or doctors or nurses, either. We had to fend for ourselves if sickness came."

In slavery time, Simon explained, only white folks had doctors or nurses to care for them. Still, if a slave became ill, he wasn't left alone to suffer unattended. In time of illness or other trouble, fellow slaves would "turn in and help out."

After the field work was done for the day, men would cut wood for the sick person and pile it up near his fireplace. Since the slaves did not have stoves, their fireplaces kept the cabins warm and also served for cooking. Usually the chimneys were wide and built of mud and sticks, interlocked at the four corners, and the hearths were big enough to hold three-foot logs.

The people hung their iron pots over the fire by means of hangers, or cranes, that swung in and out. Or they perched the pot on two level burning logs, or on dog irons if they could afford them. Some people also had pothooks for lifting hot pots off the fire. For cooking hoecake or biscuits, they used a four-legged frying pan that they called a spider. They placed the spider over hot coals in the hearth, covered the bread with an iron lid, then placed hot coals on the lid. The bread soon browned, bottom and top. If the family did not own a skillet, they baked their bread on a clean hot spot in the fireplace and covered it with ashes. When done, the ashcake was dusted off and eaten. I have eaten it myself, and it tasted good.

If the woman of a slave family fell ill, other black women came to tend the children, cook the meals, wash the clothes, or do other necessary chores. In those days, said Simon, people had love and compassion in their hearts for one another. "It wasn't like today, when everybody seems to be trying only to get the dollar. Women would come over just to sit a spell and sing and pray around the sickbed. Nobody was left to suffer alone. Sometimes a man or woman with a healing touch would brew an herb tea, mix a poultice, or apply peach tree leaves to a fevered brow, to help the sick get well. And all this loving care cheered up the troubled soul, whether he got well or died."

Simon then told me of an old slave woman named Dicey and how much her friends cared about her.

Sister Dicey was as good a soul as ever lived. She was the friend of all the folks, black and white. One day Sister Dicey passed away in her sleep. Now, the slaves

had no undertakers, so the womenfolk came in and prepared her body for burial, which had to be done in twenty-four hours. After bathing her, they put on her the best dress they could find and laid her out in a homemade coffin, resting on two chairs. Somebody pinned a flower on her bosom.

Later that night slaves from all about came to the cabin and sat around while they sang and prayed. People kept coming and going all night long. The singing was mostly sad songs with happy endings, because the folks felt that now Sister Dicey was freed from all the trials and tribulations of slavery and was safe in Heaven, at rest and in peace forevermore. She wouldn't be a barefoot slave dressed in rags anymore. In God's Heaven, she'd have everything she needed to make her happy. The mourners at Sister Dicey's sitting up knew this and sang:

I got shoes, you got shoes—
All God's children got shoes.
When I get to Heaven
I'm going to put on my shoes
And walk all over God's Heaven.

I got a robe, you got a robe—
All God's children got a robe.
When I get to Heaven
I'm going to put on my robe
And shout all over God's Heaven.

I got wings, you got wings—
All God's children got wings.
When I get to Heaven
I'm going to put on my wings
And fly all over God's Heaven.

I got a crown, you got a crown—
All God's children got a crown.
When I get to Heaven
I'm going to put on my crown
And wear it all over God's Heaven.

I got a harp, you got a harp—
All God's children got a harp.
When I get to Heaven
I'm going to play on my harp
And play all over God's Heaven.

So, with this picture of Heaven in mind, the mourners weren't too sad at Sister Dicey's going away. They knew she was better off with a loving Heavenly Father than she had ever been in this wicked world of slavery. Some of the people got so happy thinking about Heaven that they burst out crying and shouting for joy. And so the sitting up went on all night.

The next morning old Master John Brown came over to the cabin to pay his last respects to Sister Dicey, his faithful servant, and to tell the people that he would let them off from work to go to the funeral. They could use a pair of mules and his best farm wagon to carry the coffin through the woods to the graveyard.

The coffin was a plain pine box built by a good slave carpenter on the plantation who could make them to fit any size body—man, woman, or child. I didn't walk with the coffin and the mourners out to the graveyard because I was about thirteen years old and had been sent to help some of the men dig the grave. It was six feet long, three feet wide, and six feet deep. But I didn't help with the last of the digging. I was too scared to stay in the grave when it got down past my head.

When the family and mourners reached the burying grounds, six men carried the coffin to the grave and rested it on two long-handled shovels. Then they put plowlines under each end and let it down easy-like into the hole. A box lid was let down with the same ropes and fitted in place, and then a man climbed into the grave and screwed the lid on.

When this was done, the slave preacher said words of

comfort over the body—something like this: "Sister Dicey, since God in His mercy has taken your soul from earth to Heaven and out of your misery, I commit your body to the ground, earth to earth, ashes to ashes, dust to dust, where it will rest in peace. But on that Great Getting Up Morning, when the trumpet of God shall sound to wake up all the dead, we will meet you in the skies and join the hosts of saints who will go marching in. Yes, we want to be in that number, Sister Dicey, when the saints go marching in."

Before the preacher could finish his Benediction, some of the women got so happy that they drowned him out with their singing and handclapping and shouting. Then some men and boys began to fill up the grave. When it was full, they rounded it up real pretty-like and put one wood shingle at the head and another at the foot of the grave. The womenfolk laid some flowers and ribbon grass on top and put colored bottles, broken glass, and seashells all around the grave of Sister Dicey.

In that way, they showed their love for her. It was the best that slaves could do in those days, when everybody was poor and owned by their masters. But no man could own their souls or keep them from loving one another. These gifts came only from God.

Simon Sees a Ghost

ONE SUNDAY AFTERNOON I walked with Simon Brown in the "white folks' cemetery" close by my home in Society Hill, South Carolina. In those days, children were not allowed to play games or sing "worldly songs" on Sundays, but they were permitted to walk in the cemeteries. I suppose people felt that this environment would encourage sober thoughts.

The Welsh Neck Baptist Church graveyard dated back to Colonial days—to 1736. Its walks were gravel-covered and well-kept. Tall cedars lined the outer boundaries, and small flat cedars, sweet shrubs, holly bushes, and various other evergreens and flowering plants bordered the walks. In the spring, the fragrance of honeysuckle and wisteria, which climbed like serpents around the old cedars, could be smelled before entering the grounds.

Of all the ancient tombstones, by far the most mysterious and spooky to children were the marble-covered vaults. They were brick enclosures with walls rising from the grave bottom to two feet above ground. A heavy marble slab formed the top. Carved in the slab were the name, dates of birth and death of the deceased, and sometimes a brief history of his or her achievements. Most children were afraid to get close enough to read the lettering because they imagined that the skeletons inside might rattle or that a huge rattlesnake guarded the tomb.

"Yes, Willie, there might be big rattlers in some of these graves, because there're holes around them," remarked Simon. "Then, too, I've seen some mighty wide snake tracks in the sand leading from the graveyard. So don't ever go near these tombs at night."

The old man then lowered his voice and said, "You know, I was born with a caul (fetal membrane) over my face, and that gave me the power to see ghosts. I can see spirits moving around when other folks can't. But they don't ever bother me. My grandmama used to tell me that spirits could help you if you weren't afraid of them. She called them her 'blind god.' So I reckon I must have a blind god, too, because now I'm not afraid of ghosts. Of course, that wasn't always true. Once, when I was a young man, a haunt scared me pretty bad one night."

My eyes grew wide as Simon went on to tell me of his encounter with the haunt, or ghost.

Now, I was a sinner-man in my young days, and I didn't mind taking a drink of rum if I could get it. Slaves weren't allowed to drink liquor by law, but on this night I had a pint bottle of white corn whiskey. My mother didn't know it. She was a good Christian. Still, I had the pater-rollers to look out for, because even though I had my pass in my pocket to go see my girl on

the next plantation, the pater-rollers would try to thrash
me if they caught me with that liquor. But I got by them
all right without being seen. And I spent the evening
with my girl and some friends, eating and drinking and
having a good time.

On my way home, I had to pass a graveyard. By then
the moon was high and shining bright. The tombstones
all looked like white ghosts standing up. But I knew they
were just tombstones. Even so, I tiptoed by the graveyard,
half-drunk and half-scared. Before I passed the last tomb-
stone, I looked behind me, and there was a little white
puppy frolicking in the road.

I said to myself, "Simon, did you fetch along that
puppy?" "No, sir," I said back to myself. "He looks as if
he just came up out of the ground. Maybe I'd better sober
up."

So I turned around and yelled at him, "Scat! Get away from here!" But he didn't scat or even stop his prancing. Then, I was about to pick up a stick and run him back down the road, when I stopped dead still in my tracks. The white puppy didn't have any head on him! He was a ghost—a sure-enough haunt!

I turned around and headed for home as fast as my legs would take me. But no matter how fast I traveled—and I was a pretty good runner—that dratted puppy kept right behind me. To make matters worse, when I looked over my shoulder, that no-headed puppy had grown to be a big dog—as big as a bloodhound! And he was right at my heels to boot! I let out a yell that could be heard half a mile away and put on more speed. I said to myself, "Please, feet, help the body. Put them down and pick them up. A haunt is about to catch Simon!"

When I yelled, my mother must have heard me, because she lit the oil lamp by the window. But I was still a long way from the house. And me and that no-headed dog were a-running. Suddenly I remembered something my grandmama had told me. She'd said, "If a haunt ever gets behind you, Simon, and you've got any liquor in your pocket, pour it out on the ground, and that will slow him down. He'll have to lick it up, a drop at a time." With that, I pulled out the whiskey bottle and emptied it on the ground as I ran. But that didn't help a bit. That danged hound dog just kept on a-coming, right behind me.

Then I looked back again, and I must have jumped two feet! That no-headed dog had turned into a full-grown steer with horns on his head! And he was galloping with his head down as if he meant business. Yet I couldn't hear his feet hitting the ground nor his snorting like a mad bull.

"Lordy," I cried, "this is a sure-enough ghost, and he's going to catch me on his horns! Please, Lord, don't let the Devil get me!"

By that time, I was almost in my yard, running like a deer. "Mama, Mama, please fling open the door!" I yelled. She opened the door, but me and the ghost were running so fast I couldn't duck in. "Hold it open until I come around the house," I hollered. I cut around the house, but didn't slow down. The bull was gaining on me. Just as I thought I could make it to the door, he caught me in the seat of my pants and pitched me plumb through the door, flat on my face at my mama's feet. At least I thought so.

Boy, did my mama give me a tongue-lashing! She said, "Whatever it was that was chasing you, I thank the Lord for it, whether it was a ghost or old Satan himself—because you have been drinking. I can smell the liquor on your breath. Let this be a lesson to you, and don't touch that poison stuff again! I hope that ghost scared you sober for the rest of your life."

And I reckon Mama got her wish, because I never cared for liquor after that.

Simon told me many other ghost stories, and a couple times he even wanted to show me some "sure-enough haunts." I remember once when he dared me to look at a ghost he saw standing in our side gate. He told me, "Go in the kitchen and bring a spoonful of salt, and we'll go out on the piazza and look at the gate that opens toward the white folks' cemetery. Then you must turn around three times and throw the salt over your left shoulder. After that, look at the gate, and you'll see a little girl with no head on." I was too scared to try.

Another time, Simon offered to wake me at midnight on a bright moonlit night and take me out of that side gate. He wanted to show me a woman ghost dressed in a white gown walk from the Welsh Neck Baptist Church to the Episcopal graveyard across the pasture from our store. He declared he could hear the rustling of her gown as she passed by. Again I was afraid to go with him.

It seemed best to leave the actual ghosts to Simon. I wanted to meet them only through his stories.

The Ways of a Witch

ALTHOUGH SIMON BROWN believed in ghosts and spirits, he never talked much about witches and conjuring, or casting spells. He had an old friend, named Calvin Easterling, however, who knew a lot about witches. In fact, he took pleasure in telling small boys just how witches behaved at night. So Simon promised to take me up into Chesterfield County one day to meet Mr. Easterling, who had been a slave in South Carolina. When I shivered at the prospect, Simon told me not to be afraid of the old fellow, because he wasn't a witch himself and didn't have the power to cast spells on anybody.

"Calvin Easterling couldn't even put a hand on you (hypnotize you) if he tried," said Simon. "The Devil never showed him how."

Nevertheless, I felt more and more uneasy the closer we got to the Easterling place up in the sand hills.

"Calvin's got a heap of scuppernongs (brown grapes) on his farm, Willie, and if you act nice and mannersable when you meet him, he might give you a bucketful."

This good news made me feel better.

Calvin Easterling's farm was fenced with rails, Abra-ham Lincoln style. I smelled the grapes before we reached his house on the top of a hill. It was a one-room log cabin, with a wide mud-and-sticks chimney at one end. Smoke curled up out of it. Mr. Easterling lived alone.

"Howdy, folks," he called as we neared his door. "Glad to see you, Simon, and the youngun you got with you. What's his name?"

"He's Mrs. Faulkner's youngest boy, Willie," answered Simon. "He pestered me until I just had to fetch him up here to meet you. Somebody at his mother's store told him how bad the witches have been treating you, and he wanted to hear whether it's truc or not."

"Sure for certain it's true, son. Just you-all come in the house for a spell, and I'll tell you how bad that old Hessian, Liz Freda, has been a-treating me. She lives down on Joy Hewitt's place near Society Hill. But it's no trouble for that old witch to fly over here at night and devil my milk cow and my old mule. You just look out the door at my cow. Look at the cockleburs in her tail and at how her bag's all shrunk up. She used to give two gallons of milk a day. But since that old witch has been a-riding her at night, the poor creature gives less'n a pint at milking."

I saw something boiling in a tin can in Mr. Easterling's fireplace, and ventured to ask what it was.

He replied angrily, "Why, I'm melting a silver bullet for my musket. That old witch comes to my spring every morning, and she looks like a rabbit, a-sitting there looking at my drinking water. Yesterday I leveled down at that rabbit with my gun and shot a hole plumb through its hide, but when I went to pick it up, it wasn't there. It ain't nothing but a haunt from old Liz Freda. But I'm a-going to get it in the morning. I'm going to shoot it with my silver bullet. Lead can't kill a haunt, but silver can."

I asked Calvin Easterling how a person could become a witch. "I understand a witch has the power to become invisible so nobody can see him move around. I hear he can change himself into anything he wants to."

"Yes, that's so," said the old man. "But if you ever decide you want to be one, you'll have to sell your soul to the Devil first."

"How can you do that if you don't know where the Devil is or how to talk to him?" I asked.

Mr. Easterling cocked his head and looked hard at me.

"Well, let me tell you how to become a witch first, and then you can make up your mind."

I sat on the floor by the hearth and listened—fearful but fascinated.

Now, there was an old woman who lived up in these hills who wanted to be a witch. She lived in a two-room log house with her brother. She stayed in one room, and he stayed in the other. One day she went down to the woods and looked around until she found a hollow stump with water in the middle of it. That's the first thing you must do—find a stump with water in it.

Then the old woman went down to the cornfield and

found an ear of Indian corn—the kind with different
colored grains on the cob, red and blue and yellow and so
forth. Then, every Friday after that, she shelled off one
grain of Indian corn and carried it down to the woods
and put it on the edge of the hollow stump. Pretty soon a
jaybird came down and picked up that grain of corn
and flew away to the Devil to give it to him. The jaybird
told the Devil the old woman's name and where her
house was. In this way, the Devil knew she wanted to see
him. But nobody except that old jaybird knew where the
Devil lived. And he wouldn't tell nobody!

It took the old woman seven weeks to send for the
Devil—one grain of corn every Friday for seven weeks.
When the jaybird carried him that last grain of corn on
that last Friday, poof!—the Devil appeared in the old

woman's room! He was dressed in red from head to foot, and two little horns stuck out of the front of his head.

"You sent for me?" the Devil asked with his forked tongue. "What do you want? What do you want?"

"I-I-I want to be a witch, Mr. Devil," the old woman answered, almost scared to death.

"All right," said the Devil. "But you will have to sell me your soul first."

"Yes, sir, I will, if you will give me the power to change myself into a bird or beast and fix me so nobody can see me when I move around."

"I'll do that and more," promised the Devil. "But remember, your soul belongs to me, and I can come for you anytime I take a notion. Good-bye!" And poof!—he was gone.

Late that same night, when her brother was sound asleep, the old woman stood in the middle of her room and took off her nightgown. Then she said, "Skin, skin, drop off me!" and her skin dropped off. She picked it up and hung it on a peg. Then she said, "Skeeter, skeeter, come here to me," and before you could wink your eyes, the old woman had turned into a skeeter (mosquito). And she flew through the keyhole, zing!—just like that.

When the old woman flew around the yard, she said, "Hootin' owl, hootin' owl, come here to me." And the next minute there she was, a great big hootin' owl. Then she flew away over the fields and houses and into sleeping people's cow lots and barns. And all through the night that old Hessian meddled with the horses and mules and cows, putting cockleburs in their tails and manes and tying them in knots.

Then, just before daybreak, the old woman came back home and changed herself from an owl to a skeeter, flew through the keyhole into her room and changed to herself again. She took down her skin from the peg and said, "Skin, skin, come here to me." Then she jumped in her skin, put on her nightgown, and crawled in her bed.

Now, this went on for many a week until one night the old woman's brother peeped through a crack and saw and heard all the curious things going on. He knew then that his sister was a witch. So, when she was gone, he went in her room and sprinkled salt and pepper inside her skin.

When the old woman returned from her mischief, she took down her skin and said, "Skin, skin, come here to me," and she jumped in it. But the skin burned her, and she jumped out again. "Skin, skin, don't you know me?" she cried.

Just then, a great ball of fire came a-roaring through the window and caught the old woman up and roared out the door with her, poof!—and the Devil's voice was heard to say, "Old woman, I have come for your soul!"

No one in the cabin stirred for a moment.

Then Mr. Easterling whispered, "Now, Willie, would you like to become a witch?"

"No, siree," I gasped. "I'd be happy if I could just have a few of your scuppernongs, Mr. Easterling."

How the Slaves Worshipped

IN THE STORY OF THE GHOST that chased him home, Simon Brown had told me he'd been a sinner-man in his younger days. If he had been a Christian, he said, he would not have drunk "strong drink," and the ghost would not have pestered him.

I thought about that, and some days later I asked Simon if he had joined the church after his fright with the ghost. He shook his head, eased back in his rocker the way he did when he had a long story to tell, and began to describe how people worshipped in slavery times.

No, Willie, I didn't join the church just then. I was too proud and maybe too much of a man to pretend something I didn't believe in. I never did trust hypocrites, and I never wanted to be one myself. And I saw so much pretending in the white man's religion that I felt better off being an honest sinner. All the Christian masters and mistresses I ever knew, and some of the overseers too, always told the black folks to be "good and obedient servants" because the Lord loved them and didn't want them to be bad. But I never knew one of these same God-fearing people to say, "Simon, we love you as a child of God, and we will treat you as a brother in Christ." So I wondered what kind of God they were serving.

Sundays I used to drive my master's family to church in town in the two-horse surrey. At the church, I had to sit upstairs with the other slaves. We acted as if we enjoyed the services, but we didn't. Sometimes, though, we liked to listen to the preacher read stories from the Bible, especially those about the brave men like Moses and Joshua and Samson. When the Bible told how Moses made old King Pharaoh turn all the Hebrew slaves loose away down in Egypt land, we black slaves thought we must be like those Jews in God's sight. And one day God would send a mighty man into our slave land and set us all free. Now, that kind of God I could love and serve. But the white preacher in his sermons never did say a word about God setting the black man free. No, sir, not a word. So I didn't put much faith in the white man's religion.

But the slaves had their Christian religion, too, and it wasn't cold and proper, like in the white folks' church. The fact is, as I told you before, the black folks in my day didn't even have a church. They met in a cabin in the cold weather, and in the summertime, they gathered outdoors under a tree or a brush arbor. Sometimes the white preacher would talk at our meetings about being "good servants" to our masters and about going to Heaven when we died. Mostly that was all he talked about.

But, oh my, when our people got together alone to worship God, the Spirit would move in the meeting! The folks would sing and pray and testify and clap their hands, just as if God was right there in the midst of them. He wasn't way off up in the sky. He was a-seeing everybody and a-listening to every word and a-promising to let His love come down. Sometimes our people were so burdened down with their trials and tribulations and broken hearts that they'd break down and cry like babies or shout until they fell down as if they were dead. Yes, sir, there was no pretending in those prayer meetings. There was a living faith in a just God Who would one day answer the cries of His poor black children and deliver them from their enemies. But the slaves never said a word to their white folks about this kind of faith.

Yet and still, I refused to confess Christ unto the salvation of my soul. Maybe it was the way the old folks went about converting me. On some big plantations, the slaves were allowed to hold revival meetings, or protracted meetings, for a few nights during laying-by time. This happened in July or August after the cotton and corn had grown up but before they were ready to be gathered. The slaves called this the laying-by, or rest time, of the crops. Of course, the pater-rollers were on hand to keep watch against any uprisings when a heap of slaves came together for religious purposes.

If the meeting was in a house or under a tree, men would make seats by laying boards on logs or blocks, and there was always a mourners' bench up front. The slave preacher or leader would call for the sinners to come forward and sit on the mourners' bench, right in front of him where he could preach straight at them. He would call out each one's sins to his or her face. Now, if a man was a gambler, the preacher'd say, "Gambler, you better get ready; you got to die." And when he got through picturing the poor sinners a-suffering in the fires of everlasting torment, he'd command them all to "fall on your knees at the mourners' bench and pray to be saved before you die."

Then the good sisters and brothers would begin to sing and clap their hands over all the mourners and try to help them to "come through"—that is, to be converted and confess their sins. One of the favorite spirituals was:

> Sister (or brother), you better get ready;
> You got to die, you got to die.
> It may not be today or tomorrow;
> You never know the minute or the hour;
> But you better get ready, you got to die!

Then somebody would pray out loud over each sinner to help him "see the light" or "hear a voice saying your sins are forgiven." If the mourner "fell under conviction" while he was on his knees, he was expected to stand up at once and "give his experience of conversion." Then there would be great rejoicing and shouting among the people, all because John or Jim or Tillah had been "prayed through." The sinner was saved at last.

Sometimes some sinners had such a hard time "coming

through" that the singing and praying would go on all night. A beautiful song was written just for these protracted revivals, and it went like this:

> I've been in the valley praying all night,
> All night—all night,
> All night—all night.
> Give me a little more time to pray.
> I've been in the valley mourning all night,
> I've been in the valley mourning all night,
> I've been in the valley mourning all night.
> Give me a little more time to pray.

Now, after the revival meeting, everyone looked forward to the baptizing. Usually the new converts were made ready for baptizing the next-coming First Sunday, down by the Mill Pond. Long white gowns, for both men and women, were prepared beforehand. And when Sunday morning came, such a pretty sight you never saw before. The folks would get their passes and come from all around—on foot, in buggies and carts, and on muleback. The candidates for baptism would gather together and march down the big road to the edge of the pond, where they'd wait for the service to begin.

One of the deacons, holding a long staff built like a cross, would start things off. Then the congregation would begin to sing a baptizing song, such as:

> Go down to the River of Jordan, go down,
> Singing Hallelujah,

Singing Hallelujah
Sing Halle–, Sing Halle–,
Sing Hallelujah.

During the singing, the deacon, who was dressed in white, would wade out into the water, using his staff as a sounding stick. When the staff reached the proper depth, he'd drive it down hard into the bottom. Then he'd go back and fetch the black-robed preacher into the water near the staff.

A second deacon would take the first candidate into the pond, to the preacher and the first deacon, to be baptized. All the while the people would be singing another song, maybe like this:

Wade in the water, children;
Oh, wade in the water, children;
Wade in the water, children;
God's going to trouble the water.

Then the preacher would put one hand behind the candidate's back, another hand on his chest, and say, "My brother, I baptize you in the name of the Father, the Son, and the Holy Ghost," and then he'd dip the person backward under the water and bring him up quickly and say, "Amen." The deacons would wipe his face with a towel and lead him out of the pond, where his family or friends would cover him with a quilt.

Sometimes a candidate came up from the water so happy that he'd begin to shout right out in the pond, and it would take both deacons to bring him safe to shore. With the spirit a-stirring this strong, the congregation might change to a song like this:

Oh, my soul got happy
When I come out the wilderness,
Come out the wilderness;
Oh, my soul got happy
When I come out the wilderness;
I'm a-leaning on the Lord.

(Chorus:)
I'm a-leaning on the Lord,
I'm a-leaning on the Lord,
I'm a-leaning on the Lord,
Who died on Cal-va-ry.

The baptizing would go on until all had been dipped— sometimes as many as twenty-five or thirty people. And the singing and handclapping and rejoicing would keep going all the time. When the last convert was brought up out of the water, the preacher would pronounce the Benediction, and people would leave for home, or they'd breakfast outdoors under the brush arbor that was their church.

When breakfast was over and the new members were dressed in dry clothes, everybody gathered together for the sermon and the Communion service at the "Brush Arbor Church" or wherever the slave master allowed them to hold their meeting. I won't take the time to tell you how our poor people carried on their Communion service, except to say it was a time of joy and sorrow. Sometimes a mother, with tears in her eyes, would stand up and confess her own sins or the sins of an older son or daughter. Then she'd beg the other Christians to pray for her and her family, that they might "hold out to the end of their days." Maybe she'd also "testify" as to how good the Lord had been to her in all of her troubles. Then maybe some member would begin humming a song of comfort for this tired soul, such as:

Let us cheer the Weary Traveler
Along the Heavenly Road.

This sort of singing and testifying and praying might go on for a couple of hours. Then it was time for the Communion. The deacons would pass the bread first, served on a shiny tin plate, and next the wine in a glass or tumbler, until all had been served. Then, just before the Benediction, everyone would rise and shake hands and sing "God Be With You Till We Meet Again." That'd be the end of the slaves' First Sunday meetings, which began with the early morning baptizing and closed with the Holy Communion late in the afternoon.

The old man continued talking for a little while, half to me and half to himself. "Yes, Willie, I was a sinner-man in my young days, but I had a heap of respect for all who got religion and who kept praying that one day I might be saved too."

A Slave's Escape

ONE DAY AFTER A HEAVY RAIN, I picked up an Indian arrowhead from a sand bed in my mother's field. I showed it to Simon Brown and asked if there were any Indians in his part of Virginia when he was a boy.

He examined the piece of flint and answered, "Yes, Willie, in my slave days I used to see Indian men come to town, mostly riding horses, on a Saturday. Sometimes Master John Brown would let me drive him to the county seat on business, and while waiting for him to come back, I'd get a chance to talk to the Indians.

"At first I was scared to get close to them, because I was told by the old folks that Indians would steal children and take them to their camps away back in the Big Swamp, and nobody could find them. You know, there were high-ground ridges back in the swamp where the Indians camped. But, finally, one day I sidled over to a young man dressed in leather pants and moccasins, and said, 'Good morning.' He was friendly and answered with a 'Howdy.' After that I was no longer afraid. Whenever I met some Indians in town, we talked about hunting and fishing and the Big Swamp and things like that. I learned a lot about how they lived. Other slaves made friends with the Indians, too."

"Did you ever go see where they lived?" I asked.

Simon shook his head and looked a little sad, as if he were remembering something regretful. "No, I never got to an Indian camp, but I knew a slave named Big Tom who did. He ran away from his master and lived with the Indians in the Big Swamp."

"Ohhh," I said in admiration. "Won't you tell me about him, Simon, please?"

Simon said he'd be "much obliged," and here is the story he told.

Big Tom was about six feet tall and weighed over two hundred pounds, and he was as brave as he was strong. In fact, it took two or three men to tie him to the whipping post before the overseer could thrash him. But no matter how hard the overseer whipped Big Tom, he couldn't break that slave in. Big Tom just gritted his teeth and took his thirty-nine lashes like the real man he was. He never begged for mercy.

Instead, Big Tom made up his mind that he was going to run away and try to live with the Indians the first chance he got. He made his plans secretly. First, one night he toted from the lumberyard a heavy plank, eight inches wide and two inches thick and sixteen feet long. He hid it under some leaves on the edge of the Big Swamp. Another night, he dug some sweet potatoes from the bank and put them in a crocus bag along with some cornmeal and smoked meat. He hid these in a hole near his cabin and covered them with rocks so the dogs wouldn't dig them up.

The night he got ready to leave, Big Tom rubbed his feet and legs with cayenne pepper so the bloodhounds would have trouble trailing him. He put a flint rock in his pocket and tied a sharp hatchet to his belt. Finally, he wrapped a thirty-foot plowline around his waist and fastened a butcher knife to it. When he figured it was too late for the pater-rollers to be riding, he slipped away, headed for the Big Swamp. He wanted to be deep into it before the bloodhounds picked up his trail.

Now, it took a mighty brave man to risk his life in the Old Dominion's Big Swamp. Even today men with guns and dogs are scared to hunt very deep in there. In my day, it was nothing to hear a catamount, or cougar, squall, or wildcats fighting at night in the canebrakes. Wild hogs and alligators and water moccasins made their homes on the ridges and in the sloughs of the swamp. And all the time old hooting owls would make chills run up your back with their loud "who-whoing" from dark till day. Still, many a slave tried to reach friendly Indians that way—and maybe find their way to the North and freedom.

Big Tom was just such a man. He knew the Big Swamp and the general direction of the Indian camp. If the dogs didn't catch up with him, he could make it there before the next night. So he plunged in the underbrush, dragging the heavy plank along. The ground soon became wet and soggy and then boggy up to his knees. He kept going until the water was waist deep. Whenever a slough was too deep, he would half-swim and half-float across on the plank. Other times he'd stand on one tussock, or island of grass, and shove the board across to another one, then use it as a bridge.

About noon Tom stopped to rest and listen. He'd been working so hard and crashing so loud trying to cover ground that he hadn't heard the barking of the bloodhounds coming through the swamp. Even if their masters, with their shotguns, couldn't follow the dogs through the briars and slush and water, he knew that a pack of hounds could kill a grown man anyway.

Big Tom had to think fast, for the dogs were hot on his trail. They followed his scent even across mudholes and backwater because they could swim. Their barking became louder and louder. He knew his time was short. He had to move fast or be torn to pieces by the big dogs—probably five or six bloodhounds weighing sixty or seventy-five pounds apiece.

Big Tom pushed his plank across to a little island that had a few cypress trees on it. He pulled the long board out of the water, propped one end against a tree, and tied it to the tree with a piece of his plowline. Then he tied the other end to another tree so that the board was just high enough for the dogs to reach with their front feet, but too high for them to jump up on. He got up on this catwalk, or platform, holding his hatchet in one hand and grabbing onto a tree limb with the other to keep from falling. He knew the masters weren't with the dogs and couldn't shoot him. So he waited.

Soon the pack of hounds broke onto the far side of the slough and bayed him, just as if they'd treed a raccoon. They looked at the water and then at Big Tom. They whimpered and howled a minute before the first dog hit the water, kersplash! The others plunged in behind him. This was just what Big Tom had prayed for —that they wouldn't all come at him at once.

The lead dog scrambled out of the water and made a wicked dash for Big Tom's feet. Big Tom was ready. With one mighty swing of his hatchet, he split the hound's skull in midair. Then the next dog and the next tried the same thing, and Big Tom brained each one with his hatchet. Finally the last bloodhound came after him, but this time from behind. The dog managed to sink his teeth into Big Tom's leg and almost dragged him from his perch before Big Tom struck him a deathblow.

All six of the dogs had been killed, and there was silence in the swamp.

Before Big Tom sat down to bandage his torn leg, he threw all of the dogs into the water for the 'gators to eat. Then he fixed up his wound, ate a couple of raw sweet potatoes, and stretched out on the catwalk to rest his poor tired body. He must have gone to sleep because he almost jumped out of his skin when he heard a loud splash in the water. It was a big black bear! Big Tom grabbed up his hatchet and pulled out his butcher knife as the bear swam toward his island. Then he jumped to the ground, waved his hatchet and knife, and yelled at the bear, "So-o-ey, so-o-ey!" The poor bear got so scared at such carryings-on that he turned right around in the water, swam back to shore, and skedaddled away in the bushes.

Big Tom untied his catwalk and kept struggling through the Big Swamp toward the Indian village. Just before sundown, he heard dogs barking and roosters crowing up on a ridge in front of him. He kept on traveling until he saw smoke through the trees. He knew nobody but Indians would live that deep in the swamp, and for the first time he felt warm inside and safe from the white man.

And that was the last I ever heard of Big Tom, the slave who ran away to freedom. And you know something, Willie—I felt I could do the same thing myself. But I knew my pretty little wife, Ellen, could never make it alive through the Old Dominion's Big Swamp—and so I never tried to join Big Tom.

A Riddle for Freedom

HAVING HEARD ABOUT Big Tom's escape to freedom, I wanted to know about other slaves who had managed to flee their masters. Simon Brown had stores of such tales to tell, and one of the best was about a smart plow-hand named Jim, who "riddled his way to freedom." This is his story, as Simon told it to me.

Now, when I was a slave in old Virginia, I met this plow-hand named Jim. He was the smartest slave on the whole plantation—and on any plantation around. Well, one Christmas morning, Jim knocked on the Big House step, and old Master John Brown came out on the piazza.

"Good morning, Master," said Jim.

"Good morning, Jim," answered Master John.

"Christmas gift, Master," called out Jim, practicing an old plantation tradition.

"Oh, you caught me!" said Master John. "You said 'Christmas gift' first. So, what do you want me to give you?"

"I want my freedom, Master. Now, if I can tell you a

riddle you can't answer, will you give me my freedom?"

Master John studied for a minute, and then he said, "Yes, Jim, I'll do it." He must have figured that no slave was smart enough to fool his master.

A whole year passed by, and Christmas came again. Then Jim rode a young colt up to the Big House, and he knocked on the steps. Old Master came out.

"Good morning, Master," said Jim.

"Good morning, Jim."

"Master, would you please call your family and all the house-servants out on the piazza, and take down the horn and blow up the field hands—all for to hear the riddle I promised last Christmas to tell you for my freedom."

Well, Master John called the family and the servants out of the house, and he took the horn down from the wall on the piazza, and he blew for the field hands to come from the quarters to hear Jim's riddle. When everyone was gathered, Jim mounted the colt and began to tell his riddle. And this is what Jim said:

> "Sambo, lingo, lang tang,
> Chicken, he flutters the do lang tang.
> Old eighteen hundred and fifty-one,
> As I went in and out again,
> Out the dead the living came.
>
> "Under the gravel I do travel;
> On the cold iron I do stand.
> I ride the filly never foaled,
> And hold the damsel in my hand.

"Water knee-deep in the clan,
And not a wiggle-tail to be seen.
Seven there were, but six there be;
As I'm a virgin, set me free!"

Master John Brown's face turned red. He walked up
and down the piazza. Jim was his best plow-hand, and he
didn't want to give him up. Old Master threw his hat on
the floor, but he just couldn't answer Jim's riddle.

Finally Jim said, "I'll tell you one more time, Master,
and if you can't answer me then, I know you'll give me
my freedom, because your word is as good as your bond.
Now, here I come again with the riddle." And Jim told
the riddle once more, real fast.

But Master John couldn't give the answer, and at last he said to Jim, "All right, Jim, you got your freedom—and the colt, too, as a Christmas gift."

So, after telling the answer to the riddle, Jim rode off across the field with his freedom papers in his hand. And from that day to this, he was never a slave anymore.

After the story, Simon and I sat in silence for a moment. Then he said, "Now, Willie, you've been off to school. What was the answer to the riddle? You don't know?"

It wasn't until I became fourteen years old that the old man told me the answer. Here it is.

> *Sambo, lingo, lang tang,*
> *Chicken, he flutters the do lang tang.*

"That was just the introduction," said Simon.

> *Old eighteen hundred and fifty-one*

was the year it happened.

> *As I went in and out again,*
> *Out the dead the living came.*

As Jim went in and out of his cabin, he had seen the skeleton of a horse on the edge of the woods, and out of it had come Sis Partridge and her drove of young ones.

> *Under the gravel I do travel.*

Jim had put gravel in the top of his hat, and of course his master couldn't see it.

> *On the cold iron I do stand.*

Jim had his feet in the iron stirrups of the saddle.

> *I ride the filly never foaled,*
> *And hold the damsel in my hand.*

Jim was riding a colt that never was foaled, or born, because its mother had died in the birthing. Jim had delivered the colt alive, and then had made a whip out of the hide of the mother, the dam. Of course Master John didn't know anything about that.

> *Water knee-deep in the clan,*
> *And not a wiggle-tail to be seen.*

Jim had his boots full of water, but there was no way for his master to see the wiggle-tails.

> *Seven there were, but six there be;*
> *As I'm a virgin, set me free.*

Sis Partridge had seven eggs in her nest, but one had spoiled, so only six hatched out. And since Jim was an innocent man, he asked to be set free.

"Ah, yes," said Simon. "A lot of people think the slaves liked to be in bondage. But I want to tell you, every one of them that was worth his salt wanted to be free. And, like Big Tom and Jim, they did most anything to get that way. Yes, siree, freedom came hard and slow to us black folks, and now we've got it, we mustn't ever let it go. You remember that, Willie. You hear me? You remember that."

PART II
THE SALVATION

Black Folktales

Introduction to Part II

THE FOLLOWING BLACK FOLKTALES are all authentic narratives told to me by Simon Brown and other elderly black men and women who lived in and around Darlington County, South Carolina. The storytellers related the versions that they had heard in their own region. Some resemblance to the Uncle Remus stories of Joel Chandler Harris and to stories recorded by other folk authors will be noted. This is understandable, for folktales travel mainly by word of mouth, and as they are told and retold, variations inevitably occur. Sometimes the tales are improved upon; other times they degenerate. But always they are living literature—stories shaped by the lives of the people who tell them and the people who hear them.

One point I wish to reemphasize is that all of the folklore of black Americans—their stories and songs, both religious and secular—and their dances served centrally to sustain them as human beings while they endured bitter humiliation and extreme suffering.

A few of the tales related here are humorous, told

simply to produce laughter, add spice to life, and banish boredom and fatigue. But most have a serious purpose underlying them. Some are moral tales used to teach right and wrong and to exercise social control over children and young people. "Brer Rabbit and Brer Cooter Race" is one example of this category. But perhaps the most important tales are those that reveal the black people's hatred of the slave system, their capacity to outwit it, and their secret call to overthrow it.

Signs of unrest, dissatisfaction, and even outright protest are easy to detect in some of the longer, more dramatic tales. As the animals behaved in the stories, so the slaves were motivated to behave in their struggle to survive. Although weaponless and defenseless, the slaves, like the small animals, could at times get the better of their more powerful adversaries through cunning, careful planning, and, occasionally, social action.

Several of Simon Brown's stories of protest and social action among the creatures of the Deep Woods exemplify this point—and clearly reveal Simon's own smoldering resentment of the slave system. In "Brer Tiger and the Big Wind," Brer Rabbit (the slave) wins the support of all the little creatures (other slaves) and even the cooperation of Nature in his scheme to outwit Brer Tiger (the master) and gain food and water for the starving. In "Brer Rabbit's Protest Meeting," Brer Rabbit dares to challenge *all* of the long-tails (the entire privileged class). Although defeated in this battle, he is undaunted in his faith that one day the good Lord will "deliver us from our misery." In "How the Cow Went Under the

Ground," a third example of right against might, Brer Rabbit again gains the cooperation of his fellow small creatures in a brash scheme. But here Brer Rabbit deceives his powerful and greedy neighbor Brer Bear not just to gain justice but to retaliate.

After hearing this dramatic story, I asked Simon if it wasn't wrong for Brer Rabbit to deceive Brer Bear about his cow. The old man replied, "Willie, if you read the Bible, you'll learn where the Lord told the Israelites to borrow from the Egyptians just before they left for their freedom from slavery. But He never told them to pay those Egyptians back. You see, God knew the Egyptians had been working those Hebrew children four hundred years for nothing, and what they borrowed belonged to them in the first place. And so it was with Brer Rabbit and the slaves. Sometimes Brer Possum plays like he's dead when the hunter catches him. He lies down with his eyes shut. But just you turn your back, and that possum's gone! In the army, soldiers learn how to cover their bodies with vines and brush and such like, so the enemy can't see them. And so with the slaves. Deception was one of their best weapons against their enemy. They had to fool the man, or be killed."

Brer Rabbit Goes A-Courting

IN OLDEN TIMES, the creatures of the Deep Woods used to walk and talk like menfolks. They used to live in houses and work like menfolks, too.

Now, when Brer Rabbit was young and single, he lived in his house all alone. And, oh, how he hated to sweep it out and wash the dishes and make up the bed. So he said, "I'm going to get me a wife."

One evening, then, Brer Rabbit put on his Sunday-go-to-meeting clothes and walked along the creek to Sis Phyllis's house. Sis Phyllis had a very pretty daughter, who smiled at Brer Rabbit and sat down with him on the joggling board out on the piazza. Quickly Brer Rabbit began making sweet talk to the pretty girl.

Just about that time along came Brer Bear. He walked right up on the piazza and sat right down on the joggling board, ka-plump! And then he began to brag to the pretty girl about how smart he was, how fast he could run, how well he could climb a tree. And poor old Brer Rabbit, he couldn't say anything. All he could do was squeeze the pretty girl's hand to let her know he was still there.

Finally Sis Phyllis came out and said, "Good evening, gentlemen! I want to know which one of you intends to marry my daughter. Now, come next Wednesday night, there'll be a singing here at my house. The man who sings the best song will be the one who'll marry my daughter—and you two are invited."

"Thank you, ma'am," said the two young lovers, and they told the pretty girl good night.

But Brer Bear didn't go home. No, sir. Instead he went right across the field to Sis Mockingbird's house. Sis Mockingbird lived up in a gum tree, on the second floor. When Brer Bear knocked, she stuck her head through a knothole and said, "Who's that disturbing me tonight?"

And Brer Bear answered, "It's me, Sis Mockingbird—Brer Bear."

"What's the matter with you?"

"Oh, Sis Mockingbird, I'm in love."

"What do you expect me to do about it?"

"Please, Sis Mockingbird, teach me a song I can sing with this good voice of mine, so I can win the pretty girl's hand and beat Brer Rabbit in singing."

"Well, you just sing this song." And then Sis Mockingbird taught Brer Bear a song. Afterwards he said, "Thank you, ma'am," and down the road he went.

Then up came Brer Rabbit. He knocked on Sis Mockingbird's door, bim, bim, bim! And Sis Mockingbird said, "Who's that disturbing me again tonight?"

Brer Rabbit answered, "I'm not disturbing you again tonight, Sis Mockingbird. I just got here, and I'm in trouble. Won't you teach me a song that'll let me outsing

Brer Bear at Sis Phyllis's party next week?" Sis Mocking-bird nodded and taught Brer Rabbit a song. Afterwards he said, "Thank you, ma'am," and down the road he ran, lickety-split.

On Wednesday night, everybody from everywhere was at the party because the talking creatures had spread the news through the Deep Woods. The only one who couldn't get in the house was Sis Cow. So she poked her head through the window.

When a big crowd had gathered, along came Brer Bear. He was dressed in a Prince Albert coat, a beaver hat that looked like a stovepipe, a red plush vest, and a gold watch chain. A great big fiddle hung down his back. He thought he was the handsomest man at the party.

Then Brer Rabbit came sashaying into the house. He had on one of those hammer-tailed coats with a split in the middle, a white silk vest, knee britches, black silk stockings, and patent leather shoes with silver buckles on them. He carried a fancy little fiddle with a silver bow. My, how the girls did primp up when he came in.

Then Sis Phyllis stepped out into the middle of the floor and said, "Tonight there's a singing contest going on between Brer Rabbit and Brer Bear, and the man who sings the best song will be the man who'll marry my daughter. Now we're going to hear from Brer Bear first."

So Brer Bear stepped out in the middle of the floor and put his fiddle down. Then he bowed to the ladies and began to sing: "Biggity bam bam bam, Biggity bam bam bam. Biggity bam bam bam bam baugh!"

Some of the ladies kind of clapped their hands, but

others put their fingers to their mouths to keep from
giggling. Still, Brer Bear thought he was the best singer
in the whole crowd, and he sat down.

Then Sis Phyllis said, "Now we will hear from Brer
Rabbit."

Brer Rabbit sashayed out into the middle of the floor
again, bowed to the ladies on each side, and curtsied to
the ladies in front. Then he put his little silk handker-
chief right up to his shoulder, ran his little silver bow
across his fiddle, and began to sing:

"Oh, my father ate up the pea vine,
Oh, my father ate up the pea vine.
And the Rabbit skipped and the Rabbit
    hopped,

And the Rabbit ate up the turnip top.
Oh, the Rabbit skipped and the Rabbit
    hopped,
And the Rabbit ate up the tur-n-i-p t-o-p!"

Now, there's no use to keep on with the story, children. That same night old Brer Hooting Owl married Brer Rabbit and the pretty girl, and they ate up all the vittles on the table. After that, Brer Rabbit and the pretty girl lived happily together down in the Deep Woods—and Brer Rabbit hasn't washed one dish from that day till this.

Brer Wolf's Magic Gate

IN OLDEN TIMES in the Deep Woods, Brer Wolf and Brer Rabbit were neighbors.

So one day Brer Wolf said to Brer Rabbit, "Brer Rabbit, let's plant a garden."

Brer Rabbit shook his head. "I'm not going to plant any garden. The sun's too hot, and the ground's too hard. I'm not going to plant any garden."

Then Brer Wolf said, "Man, I'm going to put some collard greens and some turnips, cabbages, and carrots in my garden, and I'm going to have plenty to eat for the winter. You'd better not come there and try to get any of my vegetables."

"Man, I don't like those things. I eat the wild clover leaf myself," said Brer Rabbit.

Brer Wolf looked hard at Brer Rabbit, then went off to fix his garden. He marked off some land, and he dug in the ground, and he planted his collard greens, turnips, cabbages, and carrots, and he had a fine garden. And before he was through, he built a fence all around the garden, and he put a gate in the front. You could look through the gate, but you couldn't *get* through the gate. You see, Brer Wolf suspected that old Brer Rabbit might come to his garden and try to get some of his vegetables when he was asleep at night.

And sure enough, when the vegetables were all grown up and the collard greens looked nice through the gate, Brer Rabbit came sniffing around and made up his mind he was going to get some of that food. So one night, when the moon was shining bright and Brer Wolf was in the house a-snoring, Brer Rabbit crept toward the gate with a basket on his arm. When he came to the gate, he looked for the latch, but he couldn't find a latch. He looked for the hinges, but the gate didn't have any hinges.

Brer Rabbit said to himself, "Humph, this must be a magic gate. I'm going to hide myself here and wait till Brer Wolf comes back and see how he opens the gate." So Brer Rabbit got under the bushes and laid low until morning.

By and by old Brer Wolf came out to the garden gate, and he said to the gate, "Bubmeang! Bubmeang!" and the gate flew wide open. Then he went inside the garden and said to the gate, "Crimp up! Crimp up!" and the gate slammed shut. Brer Rabbit took out his little black notebook, and he wrote down the words, and he said, "He-he-he-he-he. I've got that. Now I know how to open that gate."

So the next night, when the moon was shining bright and Brer Wolf was in the house a-snoring, Brer Rabbit crept toward the gate again. And when he got close to the gate, Brer Rabbit took out his little black notebook and said, "How do you open the gate? Oh, yes, here it is." Then he said to the gate, "Bubmeang! Bubmeang!" and the gate flew wide open. When he got inside, he said to the gate, "Crimp up! Crimp up!" and the gate closed right up tight.

Then Brer Rabbit took out his knife, cut off the cabbages, cut down the collard stalks, and stuffed them in his basket. He pulled up the turnip greens, pulled up the carrots, and stuffed them in his basket. Then, when the basket was almost full, what do you think happened? Well, some clouds came right under the moon and shut out its light, and the garden was as black as midnight down in the swamp.

Brer Rabbit had to feel his way to the gate, and when he got there, he said, "How do you open the gate? I don't remember, and I can't see the words in my book. Oh, yes, I remember now." And he said to the gate, "Crimp up! Crimp up!" but the gate just said, "Bang, bang."

Hearing the bangs, Brer Wolf jumped out of bed, ran out on the piazza, jumped over the bannister, booketybook, booketybook, booketybook, and ran to the garden gate. "Who's that in my garden?" he called. "Who's that in my garden? I heard my gate slam."

Brer Rabbit stood there just a-trembling.

And then old Brer Wolf said to the gate, "Bubmeang! Bubmeang!" and the gate flew open just like that.

Brer Rabbit ran down to the bottom of the garden, lickety-split, lickety-split, and hid himself behind some collard stalks. And then what do you suppose happened?

The clouds went right out from under the moon, and the garden was as bright as daylight again. And right in front of Brer Wolf was Brer Rabbit's basket, all full of vegetables.

"Ahuh, I know who was in my garden," said old Brer Wolf. "Nobody but that good-for-nothing rabbit. Come on out, Brer Rabbit. I'm going to get you, and when I do, I'm going to fix you good." And Brer Wolf walked around the garden, but he didn't see Brer Rabbit.

Brer Rabbit was still hiding behind the collard stalks, just a-trembling. And all the time Brer Wolf was getting closer and closer to Brer Rabbit, but he didn't see him. By and by, when old Brer Wolf got real close, Brer Rabbit got so scared that his ears popped straight up on his head.

Then Brer Wolf saw him, grabbed him by the leg,

and laughed, "Ho-ho-ho-ho-ho. I've got you now, and I'm going to fix you good."

Brer Rabbit just laughed himself and said, "He-he-he-he-he. Brer Wolf, you surely are crazy."

"How come you say I'm crazy?" said Brer Wolf.

"Because you think you've got me by the leg when really you've got a collard stalk. How come you don't turn that collard stalk loose and grab me by the leg?"

Old Brer Wolf gasped in surprise. Then he turned Brer Rabbit's leg loose and grabbed the collard stalk. And Brer Rabbit ran out of the garden and down the road, lickety-split, lickety-split. And Brer Wolf never did catch him.

Brer Bear Gets a Taste of Man

ONE DAY BRER RABBIT was a-hopping and a-skipping down the road on his way home when all of a sudden Brer Bear stepped from behind a tree, grabbed him, and said, "I'm going to eat you."

Brer Rabbit cried, "Brer Bear, don't squeeze me so tight. You might hurt me. What's the matter with you, anyhow?"

"I'm hungry—that's what's the matter with me," said Brer Bear. "And I'm going to eat you."

Brer Rabbit shivered. "Hold on there; hold your horses, Brer Bear. Don't be so fast. You want something bigger and better than me to eat, something like a man."

"What does a man look like, and what does a man taste like?" asked Brer Bear.

"A man tastes a whole lot better than a rabbit. And if you ever ate a man, you'd never want to eat a rabbit any more."

"Brer Rabbit, you'd better show me a man right quick," said Brer Bear.

"All right," said Brer Rabbit. "Let's go on down the road, and I'll show you a man."

So they went on down the road, and pretty soon they saw an old man walking with a stick.

Brer Bear said, "Is that a man?"

Brer Rabbit said, "No, that's not a man. He was a man once, but he's a child now."

Pretty soon a little girl came down the road.

Brer Bear said, "Is that a man?"

Brer Rabbit said, "No, that's not a man. That's a man's child; that's what she is."

So they passed on.

Brer Bear said, "You'd better find me a man pretty soon, Brer Rabbit, because I'm getting hungrier and hungrier, and I'm going to eat you."

"Just hold on a while longer, Brer Bear," said Brer Rabbit. "There might be a man coming along sooner than you expect."

Just about that time, away down the road, Brer Rabbit saw a farmer coming along with a double-barrel shotgun on his shoulder.

Brer Bear said, "Is that a man?"

Brer Rabbit said, "Yes, sir, Brer Bear, that's a sure-enough man." Then he said, "Now, look-a-here, Brer Bear, all you have to do is go right on up to that man and begin eating him. You'll find he'll taste mighty good. Oh, by the way, while you're eating the man, I'm going to step on over to the other side of the thicket there. I'll be waiting for you when you're through."

So Brer Rabbit rushed through the thicket, lickety-

split, lickety-split, and sat down on a little tussock to wait for what he knew he was going to hear.

Pretty soon the gun sounded. "Bluuuump! Bluuuump!" And Brer Bear came tearing through the thicket as if something terrible was chasing him, and he was just a-raring and a-roaring.

"It's time for me to make tracks for home in the gum tree," Brer Rabbit said to himself. And so he went down the road, lickety-split, lickety-split, with Brer Bear right behind him. Brer Rabbit jumped in the hole in his tree, slammed the door in Brer Bear's face, and then crept up and looked through a knothole.

"Brer Bear, how did the man taste?" asked Brer Rabbit.

Brer Bear said, "I don't know how he tastes, and I

don't want to know, because that stick he carried on his shoulder shot out thunder and lightning that filled my hide full of red-hot fire."

And Brer Rabbit said, "Well, Brer Bear, I guess you'd better not trust a man. And you'd better not believe everything you hear either."

Brer Tiger and the Big Wind

IN OLDEN DAYS, the creatures used to plow in the fields and plant their crops the same as menfolks. When the rains came, the crops were good. But one year no rain came, and there was a famine in the land. The sun boiled down like a red ball of fire. All the creeks and ditches and springs dried up. All the fruit on the trees shriveled, and there was no food and no drinking water for the creatures. It was a terrible time.

But there was one place where there was plenty of food and a spring that never ran dry. It was called the Clayton Field. And in the field stood a big pear tree, just a-hanging down with juicy pears, enough for everybody.

So the poor hungry creatures went over to the field to get something to eat and something to drink. But a great big Bengal tiger lived under the pear tree, and when the creatures came nigh, he rose up and said, "Wumpf! Wumpf! I'll eat you up. I'll eat you up if you come here!" All the creatures backed off and crawled to the edge of the woods and sat there with misery in their eyes, looking at the field. They were so starved and so parched that their ribs showed through their hides and their tongues hung out of their mouths.

Now, just about that time, along came Brer Rabbit, just a-hopping and a-skipping, as if he'd never been hungry or thirsty in his life.

"Say, what's the matter with you creatures?" asked Brer Rabbit.

"We're hungry and thirsty and can't find any food or water—that's what's the matter with us," answered the creatures. "And we can't get into the Clayton Field because Brer Tiger said he'd eat us up if we came over there."

"That's not right," said Brer Rabbit. "It's not right for one animal to have it all and the rest to have nothing. Come here. Come close. I'm going to tell you something." And Brer Rabbit jumped up on a stump so that all could see him as they crowded around. When Brer Rabbit had finished whispering his plan, he said, "Now, you-all be at your posts in the morning; everyone be there before sunup."

The first animal to get to his post was Brer Bear. Before daybreak, he came toting a big club on his shoulder and took his place alongside an old hollow log. The next creature to arrive was Brer Alligator Cooter, a snapping turtle, who crawled in the hollow log. Then Brer Turkey Buzzard and Brer Eagle and all the big fowls of the air came a-sailing in and roosted in the tops of the tall trees. Next to arrive were the tree-climbing animals, like Brer Raccoon and his family and Sis Possum and all her little ones. They climbed into the low trees. Then followed the littler creatures, like Brer Squirrel, Brer Muskrat, Brer Otter, and all kinds of birds. They all took their posts and waited for Brer Rabbit.

Pretty soon, when the sun was about a half hour high, along came Brer Rabbit down the big road with a long grass rope wrapped around his shoulder. And he was just a-singing. "Oh, Lord, oh, Lord, there's a great big wind that's a-coming through the woods, and it's going to blow *all* the people off the earth!" And while he was singing his song, a powerful noise broke out in the woods.

There was Brer Bear a-beating on the hollow log with all his might, bic-a-bam, bic-a-bam, bic-a-bam, bam, bam! Inside the log Brer Cooter was a-jumping, bic-a-boom, bic-a-boom, bic-a-boom, boom, boom. Brer Turkey Buzzard, Brer Eagle, and Brer Chicken Hawk were a-flapping their wings and a-shaking the big trees, and the trees were a-bending, and the leaves were a-flying. Brer Raccoon and Sis Possum were stirring up a fuss in the low trees, while the littler creatures were a-shaking all the bushes. And on the ground and amongst the leaves the teeny-weeny creatures were a-scrambling around. All in all it sounded like a cyclone was a-coming through the woods!

All this racket so early in the morning woke Brer Tiger out of a deep sleep, and he rushed to the big road to see what was going on. "What's going on out there, huh?" he growled. "What's going on out there?"

All of the creatures were too scared to say anything to Brer Tiger. They just looked at him and hollered for Brer Rabbit to "Tie me! Please, sir, tie me!"

Now, all this time Brer Rabbit just kept a-hollering, "There's a *great* big cyclone a-coming through the woods that's going to *blow* all the people off the earth!" And the animals just kept a-making their noise and a-hollering, "Tie me, Brer Rabbit. Tie me."

When Brer Rabbit came around by Brer Tiger, Brer Tiger roared out, "Brer Rabbit, I want you to tie me. I don't want the big wind to blow *me* off the earth!"

"I don't have time to tie you, Brer Tiger. I've got to go down the road to tie those other folks to keep the wind from blowing *them* off the earth. Because it sure looks to me like a *great big hurricane* is a-coming through these woods."

Brer Tiger looked toward the woods, where Brer Bear was a-beating and Brer Cooter was a-jumping and the birds were a-flapping and the trees were a-bending and the leaves were a-flying and the bushes were a-shaking and the wind was a-blowing, and it seemed to him as if Judgment Day had come.

Old Brer Tiger was so scared he couldn't move. And then he said to Brer Rabbit, "Look-a-here, I've got my head up against this pine tree. It won't take but a minute to tie me to it. Please tie me, Brer Rabbit. Tie me, because I don't want the wind to blow me off the face of the earth."

Brer Rabbit shook his head. "Brer Tiger, I don't have

time to bother with you. I have to go tie those other folks; I told you."

"I don't care about those other folks," said Brer Tiger. "I want you to tie *me* so the wind won't blow *me* off the earth. Look, Brer Rabbit, I've got my head here against this tree. Please, sir, tie me."

"All right, Brer Tiger. Just hold still a minute, and I'll take out time to save your striped hide," said Brer Rabbit.

Now, while all this talking was going on, the noise kept getting louder and louder. Somewhere back yonder it sounded like thunder was a-rolling! Brer Bear was still a-beating on the log, bic-a-bam, bic-a-bam, bic-a-bam, bam, bam! Brer Cooter was still a-jumping in the log, bic-a-boom, bic-a-boom, bic-a-boom, boom, boom! And the birds were a-flapping and the trees were a-bending and the leaves were a-flying and the bushes were a-shaking and the creatures were a-crying—and Brer Rabbit was a-tying!

He wrapped the rope around Brer Tiger's neck, and he pulled it tight; he wrapped it around Brer Tiger's feet, and he pulled it tight. Then Brer Tiger tried to pitch and rear, and he asked Brer Rabbit to tie him a little tighter, "because I don't want the big wind to blow me off the earth." So Brer Rabbit wrapped him around and around so tight that even the biggest cyclone in the world couldn't blow him away. And then Brer Rabbit backed off and looked at Brer Tiger.

When he saw that Brer Tiger couldn't move, Brer Rabbit called out, "Hush your fuss, children. Stop all of your crying. Come down here. I want to show you something. Look, there's our great Brer Tiger. He had all the pears and all the drinking water and all of everything, enough for everybody. But he wouldn't give a bite of food or a drop of water to anybody, no matter how much they needed it. So now, Brer Tiger, you just stay there until those ropes drop off you. And you, children, gather up your crocus sacks and water buckets. Get all the pears and drinking water you want, because the Good Lord doesn't love a stingy man. He put the food and water here for all His creatures to enjoy."

After the animals had filled their sacks and buckets, they all joined in a song of thanks to the Lord for their leader, Brer Rabbit, who had shown them how to work together to defeat their enemy, Brer Tiger.

Brer Rabbit
Keeps His Word

BRER RABBIT is a smart man. You have to get up very early in the morning to get ahead of him. Brer Fox learned that lesson one day when he was trying to catch Brer Rooster.

Now, Brer Fox had caught all the chickens in the barnyard except Brer Rooster. And he would have gotten Brer Rooster, too, if the bird hadn't gone up yonder in that cedar tree close to the barn. There was no way for Brer Fox to get at him up there. So Brer Fox just hid and stayed out of sight, hoping that Brer Rooster would fly down to the ground.

Now, Brer Rabbit had been watching Brer Fox because he knew that as soon as Brer Fox had caught the last of the chickens, he would begin to eat up rabbits. Yet Brer Rabbit came up to Brer Fox that day, just as bold as daylight, and said, "Good morning, Brer Fox. How are you today?"

"Oh, I'm feeling kind of middling, Brer Rabbit," said Brer Fox. "How are you?"

"I don't feel too good myself, Brer Fox, but how come you look so downcast today?"

"It's because I've been trying to catch Brer Rooster all the morning, and I haven't had any luck."

"Where is Brer Rooster?" asked Brer Rabbit as if he didn't know.

"He's up yonder in the cedar tree close to the barn," answered Brer Fox.

"Oh, that's no trouble at all, Brer Fox. I can get Brer Rooster," spoke up Brer Rabbit all confident-like.

"You can, Brer Rabbit?" replied Brer Fox. "I'd be much obliged if you would."

"Yes, sir," said Brer Rabbit, "but you've got to promise me that you'll stay right here until I get back with Brer Rooster."

"You can depend on my being right here when you get back, Brer Rabbit," said Brer Fox. "I'm not going to run away. I want to eat Brer Rooster."

"I know you want to eat Brer Rooster, but still you've got to guarantee me that you'll be here when I catch him," persisted Brer Rabbit.

"What else do you want? You have my word," argued Brer Fox.

"I'd know you would be here when I come back if you let me tie your hands to the fence post," said Brer Rabbit.

"If I let you tie me up, what guarantee do I have that you'll be back to let me loose?" asked Brer Fox kind of puzzled-like.

"I give you my word, Brer Fox. I give you my word," promised Brer Rabbit as if he were hurt.

"But suppose you break your word? What then? What'll happen to me?" argued Brer Fox.

"I'm a straight man, Brer Fox. I promise you I'll come *straight* back to you," answered Brer Rabbit.

"All right, then. I'll let you tie me up if that'll get me Brer Rooster," said Brer Fox.

So Brer Rabbit tied Brer Fox's hands tight to the fence post and went off to fetch Brer Rooster. Now, Brer Rabbit knew there was a pack of foxhounds asleep in the barnyard. The hounds were lying in a circle, all curled up with their heads between their front legs. Brer Rabbit crept up real quiet to the dogs, then jumped in the middle of their circle and jumped out again in a hurry. When he bounded over their heads, the hounds leaped up and started in pursuit of him.

Brer Rabbit turned and ran right back toward Brer Fox and the fence post where he was tied. The hounds trailed behind him just a-yowling, "Yoo, yoo, yoo-ooh!"

When Brer Fox saw Brer Rabbit and the hounds heading straight for him, he yelled out, "Turn to the right, Brer Rabbit. Or bear to the left. But don't come this way. The hound dogs are going to get me."

"I'm a *straight* man, Brer Fox," said Brer Rabbit. "I'm a straight man, and I can't turn right or left. I'm keeping my word. I promised you I'd come *straight* back to you, and here I come!"

When the hound dogs got through with Brer Fox, he was a sorry sight. And, you know, he never ate another chicken or rabbit from that day till this.

Brer Possum and Brer Snake

ONE FROSTY MORNING Brer Possum was going down the road attending to his own business, when he came across Brer Snake lying in the road with a brick on his back. Now, Brer Snake is a dangerous creature; he'll bite you if you don't watch out.

So Brer Possum walked around Brer Snake. But then he heard Brer Snake holler out, "Oh, Brer Possum—please, sir—don't leave me here to die. Can't you see the brick on my back? Please lift it off."

Brer Possum looked around, and he looked at Brer Snake, and then he reached down and picked the brick right off Brer Snake's back. And then he went on down the road attending to his own business.

But again Brer Snake cried out. "Oh, Brer Possum, don't leave me in the road to die. Don't you see how cold I am? I'm so cold I can't crawl. Pick me up and put me in your pocket, please, sir. You have a warm pocket right there in front."

Brer Possum came back and got Brer Snake and stuck him in his pocket, and then he went on down the road.

All of a sudden Brer Snake stuck his head out of the pocket and said, "I'm going to bite you; I'm going to bite you."

Brer Possum cried, "Why are you going to bite me, Brer Snake? I haven't done anything wrong to you. In fact, I helped you. I lifted the brick off your back, and I stuck you in my pocket."

Brer Snake said, "I don't know. I guess it's just my nature to bite."

Brer Possum sighed. "Well, if I'm going to die, Brer Snake, let me go down to Brer Rabbit's house and tell him good-bye."

"All right," said Brer Snake.

So Brer Possum went down to Brer Rabbit's house. Brer Rabbit was sitting on his front piazza, just a-rocking back and forth. And he called out, "Hello there, Brer Possum."

"Good morning, Brer Rabbit," answered Brer Possum.

"Where are you going?" asked Brer Rabbit.

Brer Possum said, "I'm not going anywhere. I just came to tell you good-bye because I'm going to die—that's all."

"My goodness, what's the matter with you?" asked Brer Rabbit.

"I've got a snake in my pocket."

"Oh, my!" said Brer Rabbit. "What're you doing with a snake in your pocket? Don't you know he's a dangerous creature?"

"Yes, I know that now, sir."

"Well, what happened?" asked Brer Rabbit.

And then Brer Possum told Brer Rabbit how he had taken the brick off Brer Snake's back and picked him up and stuck him in his pocket, and how Brer Snake had said he was going to bite him.

Brer Rabbit said, "I can't understand that. Is that right, Brer Snake?"

Brer Snake stuck his head out of Brer Possum's pocket and said, "Yes, that's right."

Brer Rabbit shook his head all puzzled-like. "Let's go down where the thing happened, and then maybe I can understand. I can't understand it now."

So the three of them went down the road together. When they reached the brick, Brer Rabbit stepped over beside it, and then he said, "Brer Possum, where were you standing?"

"Right here," answered Brer Possum.

"And, Brer Snake, where were you standing?"

Brer Snake crawled out of Brer Possum's pocket over to the brick and said, "Right here."

Quickly Brer Rabbit slapped the brick down on Brer Snake's back, and jumped away. Then he said, "Now, you just stay there, Brer Snake. That's where poison creatures belong. And you, Brer Possum, don't you ever trouble trouble, until trouble troubles you!"

Brer Wolf Plants Pinders

In olden days, Brer Rabbit had a reputation for being the best farmer in the country. He was only a little piece of leather, but he was well put together. Brer Wolf, on the other hand, was big and dangerous. But he didn't know anything about farming. No, sir, nothing at all.

So one day, even though Brer Wolf was the enemy of Brer Rabbit, Brer Wolf said, "Let's do some farming together, Brer Rabbit, and go half and half on the work and the crop."

"All right," answered Brer Rabbit. "But what do you want to plant?"

"I want us to plant pinders," spoke up Brer Wolf, who just loved the taste of pinders, or peanuts.

"That sounds good to me, Brer Wolf. Do you want to bring the seed pinders yourself, or do you want me to bring them?" asked Brer Rabbit.

"I'll bring them," said Brer Wolf. "But I've never planted pinders in my whole life. Tell me, Brer Rabbit, how do you prepare the seeds? I want to do everything right so we'll have a big crop this fall and plenty to eat this winter."

"Well, I'll tell you what to do, Brer Wolf. You go to the store and you buy a bucket full of pinders and you take them home. Then you put them in the stove and cook them until they are real nice and brown. Next, you take them out and shell them good and clean. The next day we'll meet down in the field, and I'll show you how to plant them. But be sure to fetch along your hoe, Brer Wolf."

"All right," said Brer Wolf. And off he went to buy the pinders, or peanuts, from the store.

The next day, after Brer Wolf had roasted the pinders in the stove nice and brown and had shelled them good and clean, he went out to meet Brer Rabbit in the field.

"Good morning, Brer Wolf," called Brer Rabbit, as if he were very happy. "Did you bring along your hoe and the pinders, the way I told you to?"

"Yes, sir," answered Brer Wolf. "Here they are, ready for planting."

"Good," said Brer Rabbit. "Now, you do exactly what I tell you to do, and we'll get this planting done in no time. First, you give me the bucket full of pinders, and you take the hoe. Then you go in front and dig the holes, while I come behind you. As fast as you dig the holes, I'll drop in the pinders and cover them with dirt."

"All right," said Brer Wolf.

So he set out down the row in front of Brer Rabbit, just a-digging holes with the hoe. Along came Brer Rabbit behind him, acting as if he were planting. But he wasn't planting. No, sir. Instead, he lifted his hand to his mouth, and put the pinders inside, and ate them. Then

he threw his empty hand toward the holes, as if he were planting, and covered up the holes with dirt.

Brer Wolf and Brer Rabbit kept this up, without Brer Wolf ever catching on, until all the holes were covered up and all the pinders were eaten up.

Finally Brer Rabbit said all innocent-like, "Brer Wolf, we're finished with the planting. Now all we have to do is wait for the pinders to come up."

Then both of the creatures went home. That night a heavy rain came up and gave the ground a good soak. So the next day Brer Wolf went down to the field to see how the pinders were coming along. But he didn't see any sign of pinders sprouting! The next day and the next old Brer Wolf went down to examine the ground in the pinder patch, but not a sign of a pinder did he see. Then

Brer Wolf began to get suspicious. He thought something was going wrong. So he hotfooted it over to Brer Rabbit's house and knocked on the door.

Brer Rabbit pretended he was asleep.

"Come on out, Brer Rabbit. Come on out," hollered Brer Wolf. "I think there is something funny going on down in the pinder patch."

Brer Rabbit came out. "What's happening?" he asked.

"Well, I don't exactly know what's happened, but I do know one thing," said Brer Wolf. "There's no sign of any pinders coming up. The ground hasn't cracked open in even one place in the whole field."

"Hmm, that's funny. Let's go down there and look around," said Brer Rabbit all innocent-like.

So the two of them went down to the pinder patch together. And then Brer Rabbit ran ahead of Brer Wolf and began to dig in the pinder patch.

Pretty soon he hollered, "Oh, Brer Wolf, look here. We've run into bad luck. You know what I think? I think the ground moles came in here and ate up those pinders while you and I weren't looking. We'll have to plant us another crop."

Big old Brer Wolf looked at little old Brer Rabbit all puzzled, as if he didn't know what to do. But you can be sure he made up his mind to keep a stern eye on Brer Rabbit the next time they planted a crop together.

Brer Wolf's Second Pinder Patch

Now, OLD BRER WOLF didn't feel very good after losing all of the pinders, or peanuts, to the ground moles in his first planting with Brer Rabbit. He felt that somehow Brer Rabbit had tricked him. He didn't let on, though, because he didn't have any way to prove what had become of the pinders. You see, his back had been turned every time Brer Rabbit had thrown the pinders into his mouth instead of into the holes Brer Wolf had dug. Nevertheless, Brer Wolf made up his mind that if he went into sharecropping with Brer Rabbit again, he would watch him carefully, every move he made, for Brer Wolf just knew he had more sense than Brer Rabbit.

A few days later Brer Wolf figured he had a way to get the best of Brer Rabbit in farming, so off he went to talk to Brer Rabbit about planting a new crop. Brer Rabbit was sitting in his rocking chair on his front piazza when Brer Wolf came up.

"Howdy, Brer Wolf, howdy," said Brer Rabbit, as if nothing had ever happened between him and Brer Wolf.

"Howdy yourself, Brer Rabbit," responded Brer Wolf.

"What can I do for you?" said Brer Rabbit.

"Oh, I've just been thinking that we might try our hand at planting some more pinders, Brer Rabbit. Only this time we're going to make sure the ground moles don't come in the field and eat them up before they sprout."

"Well, I'm willing to plant some more pinders with you, Brer Wolf, and I guarantee the ground moles won't get them this time, because we're going to plant them in a new spot, some new ground, just ready for a new crop."

"That sounds good to me, Brer Rabbit. But there's a special arrangement I want to make about who gets the tops of the pinders and who gets the bottoms."

Now, Brer Wolf is much larger than Brer Rabbit, and he's mighty strong, and he's mighty greedy. But he'll have to get up soon in the morning to fool Brer Rabbit, because Brer Rabbit is a little creature with a heap of sense. He knew right away that Brer Wolf was figuring on taking the whole crop of pinders at gathering time, so that he would get nothing. And he was ready for the trick.

"What's your special arrangement, Brer Wolf?" he asked.

"I want the tops, and you take the bottoms," answered Brer Wolf, thinking that more pinders grew on the vines than on the roots. "That's how I want it, Brer Rabbit. Give me the tops."

"All right, Brer Wolf, you can have the tops, and I'll take the bottoms," agreed Brer Rabbit without even batting his eyes, for of course Brer Rabbit knew that pinders grow only on the bottoms.

So the next day Brer Rabbit and Brer Wolf met down at the new ground and planted the pinders together. And by and by, after two or three heavy rains, the pinders began to sprout, and it appeared as if the two partners were going to have plenty of peanuts to eat during the long winter.

It took a heap of hoeing and a heap of weed chopping before the pinder vines grew up and had plenty of blossoms on them. And mostly Brer Wolf did the hard work while Brer Rabbit rested himself in the shade. Then, by and by, the frost came and hit the pinder vines and shriveled them up—a sure sign that they're ripe for the gathering. But Brer Wolf didn't know anything about the frost. Only Brer Rabbit knew, because he was a smart farmer.

So one morning Brer Rabbit went down to the pinder patch and began to pull up the vines that belonged to Brer Wolf. And every time he pulled up a vine, he stripped the pinders from the roots and threw them into a big basket he had brought along. Then he took his pitchfork and tossed the tops of the vines into piles all over the pinder patch, all ready for Brer Wolf when he came down.

And, a little while later, down he came. Well, when Brer Wolf saw the great tall piles of pinder vines, his eyes grew big with greediness, and he licked his jaws just thinking what a nice juicy crop of pinders he was going to have for the winter. Then he grabbed up a handful of the vines and looked for the pinders, but there were no pinders to be found. Every pinder was gone.

Brer Wolf looked around on the ground, and then he looked around for Brer Rabbit, but Brer Rabbit wasn't there. Brer Wolf took off running, and when he reached Brer Rabbit's house, he found Brer Rabbit up on his barn roof spreading out the pinders for the sun to dry.

"Look-a-here, Brer Rabbit, where are my pinders?" hollered Brer Wolf. "There's none left on the tops down in the field."

"Oh-h-h, Brer Wolf," answered Brer Rabbit with a grin, "you got what you bargained for. You asked for the tops, and the tops are what you got. Of course, everybody excepting you knows that pinders always grow on the bottoms under the ground. Your greediness and ignorance caused you to lose your pinder crop again. But maybe come Christmastime I'll give you some of my pinders to keep your stomach company."

And once again big old Brer Wolf went home empty-handed.

Brer Fox Tries Farming Too

BRER WOLF WAS MAD AS A HORNET after he'd lost his pinders, or peanuts, the second time in planting with Brer Rabbit. And he vowed he'd get even with Brer Rabbit if it was the last thing he did.

Fuming and fussing, Brer Wolf hopped on over to see his friend Brer Fox. Brer Fox's house was tucked between some big rocks on the side of a hill, and old Brer Wolf knocked on the door as if he were going to break it down—bam, bam, bam!

"Come on out quick, Brer Fox. Come on out. That good-for-nothing Brer Rabbit has tricked me again, and I'm mad as a wet hen."

Brer Fox came out all sleepy as if he weren't awake, because he'd been out all night traveling around trying to catch something live to eat.

He said, "Uh, uh, what's the matter, Brer Wolf? Tell me about all your troubles."

"Hmph," said Brer Wolf. "You already know how I suspected Brer Rabbit of cheating me out of our first pinder crop. Well, I went into farming with that trifling rabbit again, and again he took all the pinders from me. When I got down to the pinder patch, he gave me some big piles of vines, but the tops had nothing on them, and the roots were naked. He'd stripped off all the pinders and spread them out on his barn to dry."

"How come he did you that way?" asked Brer Fox. "Didn't you have a special agreement with him in the first place?"

"Yes, sir," answered Brer Wolf, "but that's where he fooled me. Before we planted the pinders, I specified that I wanted the tops, because I thought that's where most of the pinders grew. And that smart-aleck Brer Rabbit didn't tell me any differently, so we agreed to a bad bargain. This morning he gave me the tops just as I'd asked for, and even the High Sheriff can't do anything

about it now. So Brer Rabbit's got all the pinders, and I've got nothing. That's how come I'm so mad."

"Well, all I can say is that it serves you right. You should have known better than to ask for the tops," said Brer Fox.

"Never mind, never mind," snapped Brer Wolf. "I'm mad, and I'm going to get even with that rapscallion of a rabbit if it's the last thing I do."

"Now, now, hold on, Brer Wolf. How come you don't let me, a real smart man, teach Brer Rabbit a lesson about farming?" spoke up Brer Fox. "I told you to watch Brer Rabbit. He can fool you, but there's no rabbit in the whole world that can trick me!"

"Now, look, if I can't get ahead of that rabbit, as smart as he is, how do you think you're going to handle him, Brer Fox?" asked Brer Wolf.

"Just come down to Brer Rabbit's house, and I'll show you who's the smartest," boasted Brer Fox. So the two of them went down to see Brer Rabbit.

"Howdy, folks, howdy," said Brer Rabbit when the two creatures came into his yard.

"Howdy yourself," spoke up Brer Fox, but Brer Wolf said nothing, he was so mad.

"What can I do for you gentlemen?" asked Brer Rabbit sweet as molasses.

"Well, Brer Rabbit," answered Brer Fox, "I want to go into farming with you, half and half, but Brer Wolf here says you're pretty smart and might trick me."

"Oh, no, sir," said Brer Rabbit. "I'm just a little inno-cent creature trying to make a living. I'm no match for you, Brer Fox. You and Brer Wolf are both powerful big creatures, and I hear that the bigger the head, the bigger the brain! So don't be afraid of me, little old me with my teeny-weeny brain."

"Thank you, Brer Rabbit. You're a gentleman with real manners," said Brer Fox.

"Now, Brer Fox, tell me what kind of crop you want us to plant," said Brer Rabbit.

"Well, I'm not particular about what kind of crop we plant, Brer Rabbit, but I'm mighty particular about who gets what grows up."

"What do you mean by that, Brer Fox?" asked Brer Rabbit. "You get half, and I get half. Isn't that fair enough?"

"Yes, sir, I reckon so," answered Brer Fox. "But if I farm with you, Brer Rabbit, I want the tops *and* the bottoms. Is that clear?"

Brer Rabbit could hardly believe his ears. But he said, "All right, Brer Fox. I'll plant the crop, and you get the tops and the bottoms. I understand you—yes, sir, I surely understand you."

Then Brer Fox went off with Brer Wolf just a-laughing.

Brer Wolf said, "Brer Fox, you surely are a real smart man. Your agreement has Brer Rabbit tied up tight as a drum. Ho-ho-ho-ho-ho! That's a good one. You get the tops and the bottoms, and Brer Rabbit gets nothing but the air in between. I want to see his face when the gathering time comes."

By and by the crop grew up, and the gathering time

came. Brer Fox and Brer Wolf walked down to the field in the cool of the evening to get Brer Fox's share of the crop—that is, the tops and the bottoms. There was no way, they felt, that Brer Rabbit could fool them. But early that morning Brer Rabbit had gone to the field with his crocus sacks, pulled all the big ears of corn off the stalks, and left the tops and the bottoms for Brer Fox. Everybody knows that corn doesn't grow on the bottom, and it doesn't grow on the top. It grows in the middle, and the middle is what Brer Rabbit took for his share.

So big old Brer Fox and big old Brer Wolf lost out again to little old Brer Rabbit.

Brer Rabbit's Protest Meeting

WHEN I WAS A SMALL BOY in Society Hill, South Carolina, there was much talk in my village and county about politics. I heard the grown-ups speak about the Red Shirts, the Wade Hampton Party, the Ku Klux Klan, and the Night Riders. They were saying that the Southern Democrats were taking over the government from the Northern Yankees, that the last of the black people who held public office would soon be put out, and that only white people would be allowed to vote and hold public office. Already in South Carolina some black postmasters had been driven out of their homes with their families, and in one case the home had been burned. This was particularly alarming to me because my father and mother ran the post office in our village. Lynching of blacks as a means of intimidation was rapidly increasing in the South, although none ever occurred in our county of Darlington. All of this direful talk was very confusing and frightening to me.

So one day I asked my friend and hero Simon Brown what he thought of the changes taking place and the trouble growing up around us. Although the old man could not read or write—because slaves had not been allowed to attend school—I had the greatest respect for his wisdom and judgment.

Simon gave a deep sigh before he said, "Willie, you know that folks in a heap of ways are like the creatures in the Deep Woods. They act as if they're not any better than the animals that kill and eat one another. Since the animals don't have religion like folks, they act according to their nature and not according to the laws of God. They don't have any mercy on the weak and the helpless, the way human beings are supposed to do. The powerful animals in the woods just run over the weak ones and destroy them if they can. So it is with a heap of people in this world. They don't have any more conscience than the big varmints in the woods. All this politicking and disputing that you're hearing about now reminds me of the trouble and turmoil the creatures had when they called a big meeting to complain to the Lord about their long tails and short tails."

And then he told me this story.

It seems as if at the time of the Creation, when the Lord made all the beasts and things, that He didn't give any of them tails. This was powerfully hard on the creatures because they had no way of protecting themselves from the little biting, bloodsucking horseflies, sand flies, and mosquitoes. The insects pestered the life out of the other creatures, so that they had to live in the bushes all of the time.

Later, after much suffering, the creatures asked the

Lord to give them tails, and the Good Lord did just that. Then all the creatures were happy—at least all the creatures with long tails were happy.

But by and by all the creatures with short tails began to have troubles. When the mosquitoes and the horseflies bit them, their tails were too short to brush the pests off. All they could do was run through the bushes to brush them off, and they soon got tired of that business.

So Brer Rabbit, who's always the leader, called the short-tail creatures to a meeting to talk things over. Brer Elephant, Brer Deer, Brer Billy Goat, Brer Groundhog, Brer Wild Hog, and others all met in Brer Rabbit's front yard, and there they decided to call a convention in the Big House. At this convention they would elect a representative to ask the Lord to give all the short-tail creatures long tails to brush off the flies and mosquitoes.

Brer Rabbit explained, "It doesn't seem right or reasonable that we should go on living in distress and pain from the bites and stings of those pestering flies and things. So you-all be on time for the big convention come this Saturday at twelve o'clock, and bring along all the short-tail creatures you can find."

Now, there were more long-tail creatures in the woods and the fields than there were short-tail ones. So it wasn't long before the news got around among the long-tails that Brer Rabbit and his friends were planning to hold a convention up at the Big House to complain to the Good Lord about their short tails. The plan upset Brer Tiger and Brer Lion and their friends who all had long tails.

"Who knows what might happen to us?" said Brer Lion. "We're in a favorable situation and very comfortable. If the Lord hears from those short-tail varmints, He might decide to chop off pieces of our long tails and give them to those other creatures, and that would never do."

"No, sir, we can't stand for any meeting like that," said Brer Tiger. "Let us all get together and break up the convention come next Saturday."

And all the long-tail creatures answered, "Yes, sir, let's break up the meeting. . . . Don't let the Lord hear anything about this foolishness. . . . We'll keep those short-tail creatures in their place."

Come twelve o'clock Saturday, there were so many long-tail creatures in the Big House that there was hardly standing room for the short-tails. Nevertheless, Brer Rabbit stepped up the walk to the platform to go sit in the ruling chair. But Brer Lion jumped up and beat him to it. Brer Lion sat in the chair, grabbed up the gavel, and hit it on the table, bam! And then he called the meeting to order.

He cried out in a loud voice, "Hear ye! Hear ye! I now call this meeting to order, and I want everybody to sit down. And that means you, Brer Rabbit! Sit down!" And bam went the gavel again.

But Brer Rabbit, he stood his ground and he said, "You're out of order, Brer Lion. This is our meeting—the short-tail creatures' meeting. We called it, and now you long-tails are running over us and trying to take it from us. That isn't right!"

"I don't recognize you, Brer Rabbit. I am the modera-

tor, and what I say goes," yelled out Brer Lion. "Now I want a secretary. Sis Cow, you're a good writer. You come up to the front and be my secretary."

Just as Sis Cow was about to get up, Brer Billy Goat, who has a short tail, stood up and said, "Mister Moderator, I object to the proceedings. Sis Cow is a long-tail animal, and we short-tail creatures called this meeting. I motion, therefore, that Sis Roe Deer, who is a good writer, be our secretary."

"Sit down, Brer Billy Goat! I don't recognize you," roared out Brer Lion. Bam went the gavel, and Brer Billy Goat sat down.

Sis Cow took her seat at the table on the platform, and then Brer Raccoon stood up at the back of the room and said, "Mister Moderator, I motion that no short-tail creature be allowed to vote in this meeting and that only long-tail citizens be allowed to vote."

"I second the motion," said Brer Tiger before anybody could say anything against it.

Brer Rabbit was so mad, he jumped up and down in the middle of the floor. He shouted, "Mister Moderator, this motion isn't fair! How are you going to keep us short-tails from voting when this is *our* meeting?"

Bam, bam, bam went the gavel. Then Brer Lion spoke up, "Brer Rabbit, I don't recognize any short-tail creatures in this meeting. Now, Brer Raccoon has made a motion that I recognize, and Brer Tiger has seconded it. Let's get on with the business that's before us. All those in favor of keeping the short-tails from voting in this convention signify the same by saying aye."

Then there was a powerful uproar in the house. The long-tails and the short-tails tried to drown out one another's voices. Even Brer Elephant bellowed and Brer Bear roared, but Brer Lion stood his ground on the platform. Finally Brer Lion hit the gavel on the table, bam, bam, bam!

"Quiet in the house! Quiet, I say," roared out Brer Lion. "I rule that the ayes have it, and that settles it. There isn't anybody—and I mean anybody—who's going to trouble the Good Lord about anything. Everything is all right just the way it is. We are not going to stand for any changes.

"Now, Brer Tiger and Brer Panther, I order you to clear all the short-tail creatures from the house," said Brer Lion.

But before Brer Lion's order could be carried out, all the short-tail animals, disgusted and disgruntled, held their heads high and marched out of the Big House in a long line.

Out in the yard Brer Rabbit said, "There isn't any justice in this land. The big long-tail creatures are the most, and they run over us who are the least. They don't want us to even tell our troubles to the Lord. But this time they've gone too far, for no creature can stop another creature from talking to the Good Lord. We'll just keep on working and praying for Him to deliver us from our misery, and one day, by and by, He will answer our prayer, and that's for sure."

The Tar Baby
Tricks Brer Rabbit

THE TAR BABY STORY is probably the most famous of all
the Afro-American folktales. Simon Brown told me his
version one day when he was scolding me for being lazy.

"Willie," he said, "you are so trifling that you're enough
to aggravate the heart of a stone, let alone the heart of a
man. Don't you know that everyone has to work for a
living? If you don't believe in working, something's
bound to happen to you like what happened to Brer Rabbit one day with Brer Wolf."

Of course, I wanted to know what trouble had caught
up with Brer Rabbit. I knew that he was Simon's hero
and most always came out ahead of any other creature
down in the Deep Woods.

"Yes, Brer Rabbit is a very smart creature," said Simon.
"But this time he got caught in serious trouble with Brer
Wolf—all because he didn't want to work. It happened
this way."

In olden times, Brer Rabbit and Brer Wolf lived close
together, but they were a long way from any drinking

water. They had to fetch their water from a stream down in the Deep Swamp. Finally Brer Wolf decided he was going to dig a well so he wouldn't have to tote his water up the hill. And one morning he spoke to Brer Rabbit about it.

"Let's go in together and dig us a well, Brer Rabbit. There's plenty of water under the ground, and we won't have to dig deep before we strike it nice and cold. We can put two buckets on the rope in the well, and we won't have to tote water from the stream down in the swamp anymore."

But Brer Rabbit said, "Man, the sun's too hot to dig a well. And besides, I don't need any well myself. I catch all my drinking water from the dew off the grass."

"All right, Brer Rabbit," said Brer Wolf. "I'm going to dig me a well anyway, and mind you, don't go fooling around it, drinking up my water."

"That's all right with me," answered Brer Rabbit. "I'm not going to fool around your well. I told you I get all my drinking water from the dew off the grass."

So Brer Wolf worked faithfully and dug a deep well and found nice cool water. He put a rope through the wheel over the well, and he tied two buckets to the rope so that he could draw up the water.

Now, Brer Rabbit had been watching Brer Wolf all this time. And when he thought Brer Wolf was home asleep, he slipped over to his well and drank all the water he wanted. But pretty soon Brer Wolf came out to draw some water from the well, and he found out somebody had been drinking it up. Brer Wolf started watching his well night and day, and though he watched and watched, the water continued to go down. This puzzled Brer Wolf and made him mad.

He was just about to give up when a big rain came and made a heap of mud around the well. In the mud the next morning, Brer Wolf saw Brer Rabbit's tracks. He knew then who had been stealing his water during the night, and he was mad as hops.

Brer Wolf studied and studied to find a way to catch Brer Rabbit. He scratched his head, and he pulled his chin whiskers until by and by he said, "I know what I'll do. I'll make me a tar baby, and I'll catch that good-for-nothing rabbit."

And so Brer Wolf worked and worked until he had made a pretty little girl out of tar. He dressed the tar baby in a calico apron and carried her up to the well, where he stood her up and fastened her to a post in the ground so that nobody could move her. Then Brer Wolf hid in the bushes and waited for Brer Rabbit to come for some water. But three days passed before Brer Rabbit visited the well again. On the fourth day, he came with a bucket in his hand.

When he saw the little girl, he stopped and looked at her. Then he said, "Hello. What's your name? What are you doing here, little girl?"

The little girl said nothing.

This made Brer Rabbit angry, and he shouted at her, "You no-mannered little snip, you! How come you don't speak to your elders?"

The little girl still said nothing.

"I know what to do with little children like you. I'll slap your face and teach you some manners if you don't speak to me," said Brer Rabbit.

Still the little girl said nothing.

And then Brer Rabbit lost his head and said, "Speak to me, I say. I'm going to slap you." With that, Brer Rabbit slapped the tar baby in the face, bam, and his right hand stuck.

"A-ha, you hold my hand, do you? Turn me loose, I say. Turn me loose. If you don't, I'm going to slap you with my left hand. And if I hit you with my left hand, I'll knock the daylights out of you."

But the little girl said nothing. So Brer Rabbit drew back his left hand and slapped the little girl in her face, bim, and his left hand stuck.

"Oh, I see. You're going to hold both my hands, are you? You better turn me loose. If you don't, I'm going to kick you. And if I kick you, it's going to be like thunder and lightning!" With that, Brer Rabbit drew back his right foot and kicked the little girl in the shins with all his might, blap! Then his right foot stuck.

"Well, sir, isn't this something? You better turn my foot loose. If you don't, I've got another foot left, and I'm going to kick you with it, and you'll think a cyclone hit you." Then Brer Rabbit gave that little girl a powerful kick in the shins with his left foot, blip! With that, his left foot stuck, and there he hung off the ground, between the heavens and the earth. He was in an awful fix. But he still thought he could get loose.

So he said to the little girl, "You've got my feet and my

hands all stuck up, but I've got one more weapon, and that's my head. If you don't turn me loose, I'm going to butt you! And if I butt you, I'll knock your brains out." Finally then, Brer Rabbit struck the little girl a powerful knock on the forehead with his head, and it stuck, and there he hung. Smart old Brer Rabbit, he couldn't move. He was held fast by the little tar baby.

Now, Brer Wolf was hiding under the bushes, watching all that was going on. And as soon as he was certain that Brer Rabbit was caught good by his little tar baby, he walked over to Brer Rabbit and said, "A-ha, you're the one who wouldn't dig a well. And you're the one who's going to catch his drinking water from the dew off the grass. A-ha, I caught the fellow who's been stealing my water. And he isn't anybody but you, Brer Rabbit. I'm going to fix you good."

"No, sir, Brer Wolf, I haven't been bothering your water. I was just going over to Brer Bear's house, and I stopped by here long enough to speak to this little no-manners girl," said Brer Rabbit.

"Yes, you're the one," said Brer Wolf. "You're the very one who's been stealing my drinking water all this time. And I'm going to kill you."

"Please, sir, Brer Wolf, don't kill me," begged Brer Rabbit. "I haven't done anything wrong."

"Yes, I'm going to kill you, but I don't know how I'm going to do it yet," growled Brer Wolf. "Oh, I know what I'll do. I'll throw you in the fire and burn you up."

"All right, Brer Wolf," said Brer Rabbit. "Throw me in the fire. That's a good way to die. That's the way my grandmother died, and she said it's a quick way to go. You can do anything with me, anything you want, but please, sir, don't throw me in the briar patch."

"No, I'm not going to throw you in the fire, and I'm not going to throw you in the briar patch. I'm going to throw you down the well and drown you," said Brer Wolf.

"All right, Brer Wolf, throw me down the well," said Brer Rabbit. "That's an easy way to die, but I'm surely going to smell up your drinking water, sir."

"No, I'm not going to drown you," said Brer Wolf. "Drowning is too good for you." Then Brer Wolf thought and thought and scratched his head and pulled his chin whiskers. Finally he said, "I know what I'm going to do with you. I'll throw you in the briar patch."

"Oh, no, Brer Wolf," cried Brer Rabbit. "Please, sir, don't throw me in the briar patch. Those briars will tear up my hide, pull out my hair, and scratch out my eyes. That'll be an awful way to die, Brer Wolf. Please, sir, don't do that to me."

"That's exactly what I'll do with you," said Brer Wolf all happy-like. Then he caught Brer Rabbit by his hind legs, whirled him around and around over his head, and threw him way over into the middle of the briar patch.

After a minute or two, Brer Rabbit stood up on his hind legs and laughed at Brer Wolf and said to him, "Thank you, Brer Wolf, thank you. This is the place where I was born. My grandmother and grandfather and all my family were born right here in the briar patch."

And that's the end of the story.

Run, Brer Gator, Run!

ONE DAY a fox who happened to be Brer Rabbit's friend was down by the Pee Dee River, and he saw a huge old alligator out in the river sunning himself on a big rock. After the two animals had talked for a while, Brer Gator said to Brer Fox, "I am the smartest creature in the whole world." Brer Fox said he knew someone who might not agree, and he trotted over to Brer Rabbit's house and told him what Brer Gator had said.

Brer Rabbit just laughed and laughed. Then he said, "Brer Fox, you be at the river in the morning, and we'll see how smart old Brer Gator is."

Next morning Brer Gator crawled out from the cold water and stretched himself on the warm rock. Now, in those days, his hide was smooth and pretty like a shark's skin. It gleamed as he slept in the sun, keeping one eye open and one eye shut so he could see while he was asleep.

Pretty soon Brer Fox and Brer Rabbit came down to the river, and Brer Fox whispered to Brer Rabbit, "There's Brer Gator sound asleep on the rock." Brer Rabbit picked up a rock and threw it at Brer Gator to wake him up. It hit the alligator on the top of his head.

Brer Gator opened both eyes and said, "Where'd that hickory nut come from?"

And Brer Rabbit said, "Hey, over there, Brer Gator! How are you this morning?"

"I'm fine," answered Brer Gator. "Just fine."

And Brer Rabbit said, "Looks to me as if you're sleeping on a mighty hard bed out there on those rocks, Brer Gator."

"Plenty soft enough for me," answered Brer Gator.

And Brer Rabbit said, "That's because you don't know where there's a softer bed."

"There isn't any softer bed anywhere in the whole world," said Brer Gator.

And Brer Rabbit said, "I know where there's one. It's so soft that when you lie on it you just go up and down, up and down, like this." And Brer Rabbit waved his arms up and down, up and down.

"You'll have to show me before I'll believe it," said Brer Gator.

And Brer Rabbit said, "Come on up here and I'll show you the soft bed."

So Brer Gator dove into the water, swam to the bank, and crawled up to where Brer Rabbit was. Brer Fox stayed hidden in the bushes just a-watching, while Brer Rabbit took Brer Gator away out in the broom-sage field where the grass is tall and dry—and where the day before Brer Rabbit had cut a high pile of broom grass for Brer Gator to lie on.

Now, Brer Rabbit said, "See that, Brer Gator. There's the softest and warmest bed you'll ever sleep on in your whole life. Try it and see."

So Brer Gator tried the bed, and it went up and down, up and down, just as Brer Rabbit had said. And pretty soon Brer Gator was so warm and comfortable that he fell off to sleep. And he shut both eyes.

Then Brer Rabbit crept off and crept off until he was out of sight. He ran down to his house, lickety-split. And he buckled on his hatchet, grabbed a lightwood torch and a firebrand from the fireplace, and ran back to the broom-grass field where Brer Gator was sound asleep. He set the grass on fire on the north side and on the east and on the west and on the south. That left Brer Gator right in

the middle of the field, with the fire burning all around him.

Then Brer Rabbit jumped over the fire, hopped on Brer Gator's back, and woke him up with a smack of the hatchet. "Field's on fire!" Brer Rabbit hollered out. "Run, Brer Gator, run! The field's on fire! Run, Brer Gator, run! The field's on fire!" He kept saying this and hitting Brer Gator on the head with the hatchet at the same time.

And then Brer Rabbit saw his chance, and he hopped off and jumped over the fire to safety. But he kept on hollering, "Run, Brer Gator, run! The field's on fire! Run, Brer Gator, run! The field's on fire!"

Brer Gator ran this way, but the fire burned him, and the smoke got in his eyes. Then Brer Gator ran that way, and the fire scorched his hide until it was wrinkled and scaly. By and by he saw the trees on the riverbank, and he burst right through the fire and the smoke. Then he jumped way over in the water, ker-plashow! And he sank out of sight to cool off.

After a while, he rose up for air, and he said, "It surely was hot out there! That fire ruined my pretty hide and made it all rough and scaly."

Then Brer Rabbit, who had been waiting by the river, said, "It serves you right, Brer Gator. That's what you get for bragging that you are the smartest creature in the world."

Old Brer Gator groaned and sank underneath the water to cool off. And from that day to this, all alligators have had rough and scaly hides.

Brer Rabbit and Brer Cooter Race

A LONG TIME AGO, when the creatures lived together in villages the way people do today, Brer Rabbit and Brer Box Cooter were neighbors. But Brer Rabbit used to poke fun at Brer Cooter because, like all turtles, he had to carry his house on his back wherever he went and he always moved about so slowly.

"Brer Cooter, I feel sorry for you sometimes," said Brer Rabbit one day. "You travel around so slowly on those short legs of yours that it's a wonder you can get out of a shower of rain. And you look so funny carrying your house on your back. I declare there isn't but one other creature in the whole world that's slower than you—and he carries his house on his back, too. It's Brer Snail. Ho! Ho! Ho! That is funny! You and Brer Snail are the slowest creatures in the world." And Brer Rabbit doubled up with laughter as he looked down at Brer Cooter. This hurt Brer Cooter's feelings and made him angry.

"Hold on there, Mister Smart-Aleck," said Brer Box Cooter. "Don't talk too fast. The old folks say, 'An empty wagging makes a heap of fuss.' And that's what I think about you. Just because your legs are long and you can pick them up quick, it doesn't mean you can outrun me in a footrace. In a fair race, man to man, I'll run your long ears off you," challenged Brer Cooter.

This was more than Brer Rabbit could stand. His ears were big and long, but for once he was too amazed to believe them. The idea of Brer Cooter, the slowest creature in town, outrunning Brer Rabbit, the fastest runner in town except possibly for Brer Deer, was just too much for Brer Rabbit. He rolled over and over on the ground and laughed and laughed until he looked silly.

Finally he caught his breath and managed to say, "Brer Cooter, that's too funny to be sensible. Fact is, it's impossible. Cooter outrun rabbit in a footrace? No living creature's ever heard tell of such a thing. Why, Brer Cooter, it's so impossible that I'll bet you a whole bushel of pinders that you can't outrun me. And I'll even let you lay out the racetrack and set up the mile posts yourself."

Brer Box Cooter appeared to be well pleased to run a race with Brer Rabbit. Especially since Brer Fox and Brer Wolf and other creatures of the village had come up and overheard much of the big talk, and Brer Rabbit was strutting all around the street, boasting of his speed before the crowd. Brer Cooter's pride would not let him back out of the race now.

"All right, Brer Rabbit," he said, "we'll run the race this coming Saturday afternoon, straight across the field for two miles. And I'll set up the mileposts myself."

Now, it did not take long for such exciting news to spread all over the countryside, and by Saturday morning the creatures from miles around began gathering for the footrace. Brer Cooter had laid out the racecourse very carefully, taking special care to run it across a few gullies and high places.

Brer Rabbit paid no attention to all of this, but spent his time boasting of how he would beat Brer Cooter. He went so far as to tell his wife to be on the front piazza to watch him raise dust when he passed Brer Cooter on the way to the last milepost. For, you see, Brer Cooter had placed three posts in the ground a mile apart: the first one at the start, the second one in the middle, and the last one at the end.

Everybody from the Deep Woods and the villages nearby was on hand to see the race and to root for his or her favorite. At the signal to go, Brer Rabbit and Brer Cooter dashed away from the first post at top speed. In an instant, Brer Rabbit had passed Brer Cooter and kicked up dust in his face. Brer Cooter went steadily on.

Brer Rabbit soon was so far ahead that he said to himself, "Aw shucks, I've left Brer Box Cooter so far behind, I'm going to lie down and take a nap."

And he did. And while he was asleep, Brer Cooter disappeared in a gully.

After a while, Brer Rabbit awoke and dashed off across the field toward the second post. Brer Cooter was nowhere in sight. So, as Brer Rabbit neared the post, he called out, "Hello there, Brer Cooter! Where are you?"

Instantly Brer Cooter struck his shell against the post and said, "Here I am, Brer Rabbit! I've been here so long my head is in my house." And his head actually was in his shell.

Brer Rabbit was so surprised he couldn't believe what he saw. Nevertheless, he said to Brer Cooter, "Come on, slowpoke. I slept too long back there. But you won't beat me to the last post. Good-bye, I'm gone."

With that, Brer Rabbit left the turtle far behind again as he galloped across the field. But Brer Rabbit had not gone very far before he came to his house, and then he stopped.

"Hello, honey!" he said to his wife. "I just thought I'd stop by and talk with you a bit. You see, I left that old slowpoke of a cooter so far behind, he couldn't see me for my dust."

"Come on in, dear, and sit down on the piazza for a spell," encouraged his wife. "You must be hot and tired from running on a day like this. I'll bring you some lemonade." So Brer Rabbit took a seat on the piazza and soon lost track of time as he talked and drank lemonade.

Finally he remembered the race, ran down the steps, jumped over the fence, and was off again at top speed. He looked like a whirlwind coming across the field, he was raising so much dust. Not seeing Brer Box Cooter again, he yelled out as he neared the milepost, "Where are you, Brer Cooter?"

Instantly came back the answer, "Here I am, Brer Rabbit. I've been here so long my head is in my house." And Brer Cooter rapped the milepost with his shell as Brer Rabbit dashed up just a moment too late to win the race.

So Brer Cooter won the footrace and the bushel of pinders, while Brer Rabbit became the laughingstock of all the creatures for miles around. And, strange to say, Brer Rabbit never found out that Brer Box Cooter had planted one of his cousins in the ground with only his head showing at the last two posts. When the cousins had seen Brer Rabbit coming, they'd jumped out of the ground and said, "Here I am, Brer Rabbit. I've been here so long my head is in my house."

And from this race with Brer Cooter, Brer Rabbit learned a good lesson—that it never pays to brag or to poke fun at another creature.

Brer Fox Meets Mister Trouble

BRER RABBIT MET BRER FOX one morning on the big road.

"How are you, Brer Rabbit?" asked Brer Fox.

"I'm not feeling too good, Brer Fox," answered Brer Rabbit. "Trouble's been visiting me."

"What do you mean, Trouble? Who's he, and what's he like?" asked Brer Fox.

"Brer Fox, you mean to tell me you've never met Mister Trouble, and you wouldn't know him if you saw him?" responded Brer Rabbit in surprise.

"No, sir, I wouldn't know Trouble if I met him in the middle of the big road," said Brer Fox.

"Well, I'll take you to where Mister Trouble lives, and you can meet him," proposed Brer Rabbit.

"Thank you, Brer Rabbit. I'd like to meet him," replied Brer Fox.

"Let's go, then, because I think he's still at home," said Brer Rabbit.

So off they went.

When they got close to a barnyard, Brer Rabbit said, "Right over there in that barn is where Mister Trouble stays. All you have to do is go over there in front of that door, stand up on your hind legs, and holler, 'Wahoo! Mister Trouble!' and he will come out."

Brer Fox crawled under the fence and went over to the barn. He stood up on his hind legs in front of the door and yelled as loud as he could, "Wahoo! Mister Trouble!"

And then Mister Trouble came bursting out of that barn door in the form of a passel of hound dogs such as Brer Fox had never seen in all his born days! When the hounds saw Brer Fox a-standing there, they lit out after him with such a-barking and a-hollering as you've never heard in your life. The whole kit and caboodle came tumbling over themselves as they tried to grab Brer Fox.

Poor old Brer Fox hardly got two jumps ahead of those hounds before they were on top of him as he scrambled through a hole in the fence. Two hounds grabbed his tail so hard that it broke off in their mouths, and he was a bobtailed fox from that day to this.

Brer Rabbit just stood there a-looking at poor old Brer Fox. And then he said solemnly, "Never go looking for Trouble, Brer Fox. He'll find you soon enough."

Brer Wolf Wants the Honey

ONE DAY BRER RABBIT was just moseying along the big road when all of a sudden Brer Wolf jumped out from behind some bushes and tried to grab him! But Brer Rabbit was too quick for Brer Wolf, and away he went, lickety-split, down the road. For he always said, "Trust no mistake; always jump from a bush that shakes."

But Brer Wolf didn't give up. He chased after Brer Rabbit, yelling, "I'm a-going to eat you this time for sure," and he ran faster than he ever had before. He was just within snatching distance of his prey when Brer Rabbit jumped in a hole in a big pine stump and slammed the door—right in his face.

Brer Wolf was plumb outdone, but he said, "That's all right, Brer Rabbit. You think you're smart. You think you're safe in your house now, but I'm going to get you out of that stump, no matter how strong your door is. I'm going to smoke you out. You just wait. I'll set such a fire around that stump that it'll burn you out in no time."

Brer Rabbit answered, "No, sir, Brer Wolf, I don't think you're going to do that. I've got a big jug of honey in here, and I know how much you love honey. I'm going to help myself to the sweetness right now."

"What's that you say, Brer Rabbit?" asked Brer Wolf.

"I said I've got a big jug of honey in here, which I just brought in this morning from the bee tree in the swamp. Don't you want some? Umm, umm, umm! It sure is good." And Brer Rabbit smacked his lips.

"How come you don't give me some of that honey?" asked Brer Wolf, as his mouth began to drool.

"You're welcome to it, as much as you want," answered Brer Rabbit. "Come on in, come on in."

"All right, then. Open up the door," ordered Brer Wolf.

"Look, Brer Wolf, my house is too little to hold both of us at one time. I'll unlatch the door and come out while you go in and help yourself to the honey—all you can eat," proposed Brer Rabbit.

So, as Brer Wolf stood by the door, Brer Rabbit eased himself out—smiling on the outside but scared to death on the inside—and bowed for Brer Wolf to enter his house. At this, Brer Wolf squeezed himself into Brer Rabbit's home and looked around for the jug of honey.

But, quick as lightning, Brer Rabbit slammed the door, bam, and locked it from the outside. This caught Brer Wolf inside.

"He, he, he, he!" laughed Brer Rabbit. "Brer Wolf, how does it feel to be inside while I'm outside? You were going to smoke me out. Well, I'm going to smoke you in. And if you find any honey, help yourself, while I go and get the kindling for the fire."

And so once again Brer Rabbit's wits saved his hide.

Brer Rabbit Dances for a Wife

THEN AFTER SOME LITTLE TIME, Brer Rabbit lost his first wife, and by and by he began to look around for another lady. One day he heard tell of a pretty girl who lived over by the mountain with her mother, Sis Dinah.

So Brer Rabbit dressed up in his Sunday-go-to-meeting clothes and went to meet the young girl. When he got there, however, he found two gents already sitting on the piazza talking to her. He stopped behind some bushes and looked the situation over. When he saw how pretty the girl was and heard how smartly she talked, he decided to try to outfox the other two fellows. He slipped around the house without being seen and introduced himself to the girl's mother.

Sis Dinah must have liked Brer Rabbit's looks and manners because pretty soon she was telling him about a dancing party she was planning for her daughter. She said, "Come two weeks from next Saturday, I will be inviting all the men who want to marry my daughter to try to dance the dust out of that flat rock you see in my front yard. The man who can make the dust fly will be the one I'll choose to marry her."

"Thank you for inviting me, ma'am. I'll get ready and be here on time," said Brer Rabbit.

"You better practice up, Mister Rabbit, because the fellows out on the piazza heard about the party some time ago, and they've been dancing on the rock already," Sis Dinah warned him.

By and by, the time came around for the dancing party, and the creatures from the Deep Woods and all around gathered to see the contest and to eat the tasty vittles prepared by Sis Dinah. One of the first to arrive was Brer Hooting Owl, of course, because he was the marrying parson as well as the judge. No matter who won the contest, he would tie the couple together. Next to arrive were Brer Monkey and Brer Cooter, the two courting gents. Nobody but Sis Dinah knew about the intentions of Brer Rabbit, who stayed out of sight until his time came.

When the farm bell finally rang for the contest to start, Sis Dinah and her pretty daughter came out and stood on the piazza. Sis Dinah said, "Ladies and gentlemen, thank you for coming to my party. I will grant my daughter's hand in marriage today to the first gentleman who can make the dust fly out of that flat rock in my yard. Every man will have a fair chance. Now let the music and the dancing begin!"

With that, Brer Cooter crawled out onto the rock, his shell polished to a deep shine. He stood up on his hind legs and bowed to the pretty girl. Then he began to dance, trying with all his might to make the dust fly out of the rock. He waltzed around in a circle, making a pretty sight as he glided this way and that. Next he stamped his feet hard on the rock, clunk, clunk, clunk! But no dust came up. Then Brer Cooter jumped up and down, until he remembered that he'd better not do too much of that—he might lose his balance and fall on his back. Then, when he couldn't get up, folks would laugh at him. So he just kept a-waltzing and a-waltzing, around and around, until he finally fell out of the contest. Folks clapped their hands as he crawled away.

Next to perform was Brer Monkey, dressed in a fancy red coat and green pants. He didn't just walk out. He tumbled out with two somersaults and landed on his feet in the very middle of the rock. But no dust flew. Then he stood up and danced on his hind legs and jumped up and down so high that the crowd clapped their hands. Yet no dust flew out of the rock. Next he stood on his hands with his hind legs up in the air, and he patted as hard as he could, but no dust came. Then he jumped off the rock, climbed up a big tree, and swung out on a limb over the rock. From that high perch, he jumped down right spang in the center of that rock. Still no dust. When Brer Monkey finally gave up, everybody clapped and shouted for him.

Just when the folks began to wonder if there would be a wedding since no man was able to make the dust fly, up stepped Brer Rabbit. He was dressed to kill in his hammer-tailed coat, white silk vest, knee britches, black silk stockings, and patent leather shoes with silver buckles! He sashayed out to the middle of the rock, bowed to Sis Dinah, curtsied to the pretty girl, and turned and smiled at the crowd. Then, I'm telling you, that Brer Rabbit did such a dance as those folks had never seen before. He pranced and he strutted, with his chest puffed out like a pouter pigeon. Then he did a cakewalk, with his hat tilted to one side. Next he "cut the pigeonwing" so fast that your eyes could hardly keep up with his feet.

And all the time, whenever his feet touched that rock, the dust flew! First it came over his ankles, then to his knees, and finally it looked like Brer Rabbit was dancing in a cloud. Everybody began to clap and to keep time with the music and the dance, until at last the pretty girl ran down the steps and onto the rock, where she hugged and kissed Brer Rabbit in front of all the happy folks and danced with him until the music stopped!

That same evening old Judge Hooting Owl married

Brer Rabbit and the pretty girl, and the wedding feast was enjoyed by all. After that, Brer Rabbit took his bride to his house down in the Deep Woods, and never, never did he tell anybody that he had put ashes in his shoes before the dance.

Brer Rabbit and His Riding Horse

BRER RABBIT'S SECOND MARRIAGE was a short one. Soon he was alone again, and when he began looking for a new wife, he found himself courting the same pretty girl as Brer Wolf. The girl lived up the road a piece on the other side of the creek. To get to her house, the two suitors had to cross a footlog. Each man would try to get to her house first on a Saturday evening after they had quit work in the fields and had gotten dressed in their Sunday-go-to-meeting clothes.

One Saturday Brer Rabbit was late. Brer Wolf had crossed the footlog first and was sitting out on the piazza just a-laughing and a-talking to the young lady when Brer Rabbit showed up.

"No use to come in the gate now, Brer Rabbit," spoke up Brer Wolf. "According to our bargain, the first man here is the man who stays. Now, go along with yourself and don't bother me when I'm courting."

So, according to their agreement, Brer Rabbit had to leave Brer Wolf alone with the pretty girl. He didn't like the looks of things, though—Brer Wolf seemed too cheerful.

The next week Brer Rabbit arrived at the house first and sat on the piazza with the pretty girl. But she was very quiet and had little to say. She refused to sit near Brer Rabbit, as though she were ashamed of him.

"What's the matter, my darling? Don't you love me anymore?" asked Brer Rabbit.

"I can't love any man who is Brer Wolf's riding horse," replied the pretty girl.

"Who said I was his riding horse?" asked Brer Rabbit, jumping up from the joggling board as if a bullet had struck him.

"Brer Wolf said so himself," answered the pretty girl. "He said you aren't anything but his riding horse. And I dare not love you anymore."

"I'll show you next Saturday who is a riding horse," said Brer Rabbit angrily, as he picked up his hat and paid the young lady a proud good-bye.

Come next Saturday, somehow the footlog had fallen into the creek and had floated downstream. The only way to get across to the pretty girl's house was to ford or swim the stream. A long-legged creature like Brer Wolf could wade through the water, but a little creature like Brer Rabbit would drown if he attempted it and couldn't swim.

When Brer Rabbit reached the creek, he looked everywhere for the footlog, but he couldn't find it. What would he do now? Brer Wolf would be along soon, and with his long legs he'd wade across the deepest part of the creek in safety. Brer Rabbit would have to break his promise to come a-riding to the pretty girl if that happened. And Brer Wolf would tell tales on him again and laugh at him to boot. And he might never win the girl's hand in marriage. While Brer Rabbit was thinking about all of this, he heard Brer Wolf come galloping down the big road, bookety-bookety-bookety!

Then, before you could blink your eye, Brer Rabbit fell to the ground as though he'd been shot. By the time Brer Wolf reached the creek, Brer Rabbit was groaning and rolling his eyes as though he were about to die.

"What in the world is the matter with you, Brer Rabbit?" asked Brer Wolf in amazement.

"Oh, Brer Wolf, I've got such a pain in my side I can't stand up," cried Brer Rabbit. "Unless I get to the doctor soon, I'm going to die."

"Try to get up and lean on my shoulder, Brer Rabbit, and I'll help you to the doctor," offered Brer Wolf. Brer Wolf didn't want Brer Rabbit to get to the pretty girl's house anyway, so he was glad to get him to the doctor.

"Lean over, Brer Wolf. Maybe I can pull myself up to your shoulder," moaned Brer Rabbit. Brer Wolf knelt down with his front legs bent. Brer Rabbit tried to lift himself to a standing position, but wavered from side to side like a man with the blind staggers. "I just can't stand up, Brer Wolf. And I know I can't walk. So I reckon you'd better let me down. I'll just lie here and die. Thank you just the same for trying to help me."

"No, Brer Rabbit, I don't mean for you to die. If you can just get on my back, I'll tote you to the doctor. Try to pull yourself up on my back," said Brer Wolf, who was willing to do almost anything to keep Brer Rabbit from the pretty girl's house.

"Hold still a minute, Brer Wolf, and I'll try my best to get on your back," said Brer Rabbit weakly, and he pulled himself up slowly until he half sat and half lay on Brer Wolf's back. All the while, Brer Rabbit was a-groaning and a-twitching, as if he were about to fall off in a dead faint.

Suddenly Brer Wolf felt Brer Rabbit's hands putting something about his head and ears. "What are you doing up there, Brer Rabbit?" asked Brer Wolf.

"Oh, I'm just trying to get a good hold on your mane so I won't fall off when you stand up," cried Brer Rabbit. "I've got to put this bridle on your head so I can have something to steady me when you move off. I'm so afraid I'm going to fall off with these blind staggers." Brer Wolf allowed Brer Rabbit to fasten the bridle on his head.

Then Brer Wolf heard Brer Rabbit jinglejangle something in his hands. "What are you doing up there now, Brer Rabbit?" called out Brer Wolf again.

"Oh, I'm just counting my money," answered Brer Rabbit. "I've got to pay the doctor, you know." Then Brer Rabbit fastened his silver spurs to his heels and buckled them tight. Brer Wolf was still kneeling, and Brer Rabbit was still leaning forward unsteadily on Brer Wolf's back.

All of a sudden, though, Brer Rabbit straightened up and jerked Brer Wolf to his feet with the bridle reins. Brer Wolf reared and pitched like a wild horse. But Brer Rabbit held him tight with the bridle and reins. Then

Brer Rabbit turned Brer Wolf's head toward the creek and stuck his silver spurs into Brer Wolf's sides. Brer Wolf jumped forward as if a spark of fire had scorched him.

"Giddap," yelled Brer Rabbit, and across the creek they went. Then up the bank and down the road they sped, straight for the pretty girl's house.

Brer Wolf twisted and turned, bucked and snorted, and foamed at the mouth—he was so mad. But at every twist and turn, Brer Rabbit tightened the reins and dug his silver spurs deeper into Brer Wolf's sides and held him straight on course.

"You called me your riding horse last week, didn't you?" cried Brer Rabbit, as he spurred Brer Wolf along faster and faster. "Now you see who's doing the riding, don't you?"

By and by, they came within sight of the pretty girl's house. Before they reached the gate, Brer Rabbit yelled out from the road, "Oh, Miss Liza, come to the door and see my riding horse!"

The pretty girl came to the door and was astonished to see Brer Rabbit come flying into her front yard, gaily sitting astride Brer Wolf's back.

"Whoa, my fine filly! Whoa, until I tie you up to the hitching post," ordered Brer Rabbit, who then dismounted and tied Brer Wolf so tightly to the pretty girl's hitching post that he could never get loose. Then Brer Rabbit walked up onto the piazza with his silver spurs a-jingling and a-jangling, and he was as proud as any king.

"I've come to claim you as my bride," said Brer Rabbit. "But before I do, I want to introduce you to my finest riding horse. And that is Brer Wolf."

And that very day Brer Rabbit and Miss Liza were married, and they lived very happily at her house forever afterward.

Oh, Brer Wolf? What became of him? Why, Brer Rabbit rode him back home and left him tied up at his own house until Brer Wolf's daddy came home that night and unhitched him.

How the Cow Went Under the Ground

MY OLD FRIEND SIMON BROWN used to talk about the hard times suffered by the slaves under certain cruel masters or overseers. He told, for example, how a smart field hand might manage by extra toil to grow a small vegetable patch near his cabin or raise a puny little runt pig in a pen out on the ditch bank. The vegetables and the pig offered the slave a chance to have a little extra food for his family during the winter. But usually the overseer would find out about these side efforts and order the slave to plow up his garden and plant more cotton or corn in the plot for the master, or to tear down the pigpen and turn the runt loose in the lot among the master's own pigs.

Under our system of human bondage, slaves were not allowed to own anything—not even their own bodies. And they had no rights that their owners needed to respect. It was a system whereby the strong took away everything from the weak except enough for them to exist on, enough for them to continue to work.

In remembering his own bondage in Virginia, Simon

152

said to me one day, "Willie, unless a slave knew how to outthink his master or overseer, he might not get enough to eat in the wintertime, or he might get a whiplashing on his naked back if he was caught stealing a piece of meat or something. Now, I was too smart to ever go hungry or to get a whipping. I was too much like Brer Rabbit. I used my head the same way he did. I outsmarted big old Brer Bear time and again."

And then, with great pleasure, Simon told me this tale of the triumph of the weak.

In olden times, when the creatures used to walk and talk together like menfolks, Brer Rabbit had a nice fat cow in his little pasture. She was a good milker, too. She gave enough milk and butter for Brer Rabbit's big family, and enough extra for him to divide with his neighbors.

Now, Brer Bear lived near Brer Rabbit on a great plantation, and he had a big pasture and a heap of cows. He never ran out of milk or meat. He had plenty of everything. But instead of dividing with his neighbors the way Brer Rabbit did, he was greedy. He kept everything for himself and even wanted what little his neighbors owned. He especially wanted Brer Rabbit's one milk cow.

So one night Brer Bear crept over to Brer Rabbit's farm and stole his cow. He broke down the fence, led the cow over to his barnyard, and butchered her behind his barn. Then he cut up the cow, put all the meat in his smokehouse, and nailed the cowhide to the side of his barn to be cured in the sun. He wanted to make some leather out of it later.

Now, the next morning Brer Rabbit went out to his barn to milk his cow, but she wasn't there. Brer Rabbit looked for her everywhere, and he called out her name, "Here, Betsy. Come here, Betsy," but no cow came. Then he saw the pasture fence all broken down, and he saw Brer Bear's tracks in the ground. The tracks led to Brer Bear's farm, but Brer Rabbit was too scared to put his foot on Brer Bear's land in the daytime, because Brer Bear was too big and strong for him.

So that night, with the moon shining bright, Brer Rabbit crept over to Brer Bear's barnyard, and there he saw his cow's hide nailed to the barn, and he smelled the beef curing in the smokehouse. But he didn't say anything. He just went back home in a deep study.

The next day Brer Bear came to Brer Rabbit's house, and he said, "Howdy, Brer Rabbit, howdy."

"Howdy, Brer Bear," said Brer Rabbit, kind of sad.

"They tell me that you lost your cow a day or so ago, and I'm surely sorry to hear it," said Brer Bear like a big hypocrite.

"Yes, Brer Bear, I've lost my one and only cow," answered Brer Rabbit.

"Where do you think she's gone?" asked Brer Bear.

"I don't know where she's gone, Brer Bear, unless she's gone in the ground."

"Gone in the ground?" said Brer Bear. "I've never heard of a cow going in the ground, Brer Rabbit. Are you sure you're feeling well this morning? You aren't sick in the head or anything, are you, Brer Rabbit?"

"I've never felt better in my life," answered Brer Rabbit.

154

Then Brer Bear started a-laughing to himself. "Ho-ho-ho-ho-ho, ha-ha-ha-ha-ha! Isn't that something?"

And Brer Bear went all over the plantation telling all the creatures how he thought that Brer Rabbit had lost his mind. He said, "Brer Rabbit has lost his cow, and he suspects she's gone in a hole in the ground. Ho-ho-ho-ho-ho! Now, isn't that a funny one?" Brer Bear held his sides as he laughed, and all the creatures laughed, too. They all thought that Brer Rabbit had gone crazy.

But when the nighttime came and Brer Bear was home asleep in bed, Brer Rabbit crept over to Brer Bear's house. He took down his cowhide from Brer Bear's barn and put it under his arm. Then he picked out the fattest cow he could find in Brer Bear's cow lot and led her over to his own barnyard. There in the moonlight he and some of his cousins butchered the cow, and he hung up the meat in his smokehouse and buried the hide. Finally he nailed his own cowhide up on his barn.

The next day over came Brer Bear, just hopping mad.

"Look-a-here, Brer Rabbit, look-a-here," he hollered. "I've lost one of my best milk cows. Have you seen her on your place? Now, I'll tell you, I better not find her over here. If I do, you're going to pay for it."

"No, sir, Brer Bear, I haven't seen any strange cows around here this morning," said Brer Rabbit. "But I'll help you look for her if you want me to. I know how bad you feel because I lost my one and only cow a few days ago myself, remember?"

"All right. You can help me look around," said Brer Bear.

So they both set out and looked around for Brer Bear's milk cow. Brer Rabbit went this way, and Brer Bear went the other way.

Suddenly Brer Rabbit called out, "Oh, Brer Bear, come a-running quick! Come a-running! I've caught your cow going down in a hole in the ground! She was almost out of sight, but I grabbed her tail just in time. I can't hold on much longer. You'd better run over here and grab ahold of her tail, too. Come on, Brer Bear. Come on. Come on."

And Brer Bear came a-running, bookety, bookety, bookety! When he got there, he shoved Brer Rabbit out of the way and grabbed his cow's tail with both hands. Then he began to pull.

"Pull hard, Brer Bear, or she might get away," hollered Brer Rabbit. "She might do what my cow did. She might

go down out of sight, never more to be seen. So pull hard, Brer Bear. Pull hard!"

Brer Bear braced his hind legs and put all of his strength into pulling. Up came the cow tail, kwump! It hit him so hard that he rolled over backwards!

"Aw, look what you've done, Brer Bear," said Brer Rabbit. "You've pulled so hard that you've broken off the cow's tail, and she's gone down in the ground forever. Too bad, Brer Bear. Now you're in the same fix with me. We've both lost our cows the same way."

Now, Brer Bear never did figure out how little old Brer Rabbit got even with him for stealing his cow. Brer Bear just always thought that his whole cow had gone under the ground—and nobody ever told him it was only his cow's hide that had been buried by Brer Rabbit the night before.

Who Stole Brer Gilyard's Sheep?

BRER WOLF AND BRER FOX were mighty angry with Brer Rabbit because he was always outsmarting them—in farming, in courting, in everyday doings.

One day Brer Wolf said to Brer Fox, "I wish I could get even with Brer Rabbit. I just won't have a moment's peace until I do."

"Yes, I'd like to take that smart-aleck down a button-hole lower myself," said Brer Fox. "I'll tell you what we'll do. Let's fix a way to get him in the hands of Brer Gilyard. That big old dragon would do in Brer Rabbit for sure."

"Yes, that sounds good," agreed Brer Wolf. "Let's do that. But how? You know Brer Rabbit is so scared of Brer Gilyard that you couldn't get him within a mile of his house."

"I hear tell that Brer Gilyard's a terrible-looking creature," said Brer Fox, kind of scared-like.

"He's worse than that," said Brer Wolf. "I saw him one night, and he almost turned my hair white. Of course, the most I could see of him then was his shining eyes and his blazing mouth. He's so monstrous and powerful and ugly that he only travels at night. If he walked out in the daytime, he might scare all of the little creatures to death!"

"Tell me more about Brer Gilyard," said Brer Fox. "I've never seen what a dragon looks like."

"Well, Brer Gilyard is hairy all over like an ox, but he isn't an ox. He has big eyes like saucers, and his nose is long like a yardstick, and his teeth are as sharp as a razor and as long as a pitchfork prong. Every time he gets mad, fire and smoke shoot out of his nostrils. And they tell me that he can eat a whole live pig with one swallow."

"I'd hate for him to grab me," said Brer Fox. "But I'd be glad for him to catch Brer Rabbit."

"All right, I've got a plan, Brer Fox," said Brer Wolf. "As you know, you and I have been stealing Brer Gilyard's sheep, and every time he comes out to count them, there's one missing. But he doesn't know who's stealing them. So let's invite Brer Rabbit to sing at that party Brer Gilyard's going to give next Saturday. He's asked all the creatures to come to his farm for a barbecue at night, and that way he figures he can catch the thief who's been stealing his sheep. And everybody had better come, because his invitation is like a bench warrant."

"I know," agreed Brer Fox. "But how are you going to get Brer Rabbit to sing down there?"

"Just leave everything to me," said Brer Wolf. "Now, I'm going to see Brer Bear and lay our plans before him."

So Brer Wolf got Brer Bear and Brer Fox together, and they practiced a song for the party. When all three knew it by heart, Brer Wolf went over to Brer Rabbit's house to ask him to join them.

"Brer Rabbit, Brer Bear and Brer Fox sent me to ask if you would sing with us at Brer Gilyard's party Saturday night," said Brer Wolf politely. "Because next to Sis Mockingbird, you are the best singer in all the Deep Woods."

"Since you put it that way, I'll be glad to accommodate you-all," responded Brer Rabbit, pleased with the compliment.

"Good. Then we'll all sit together at the table and harmonize on an easy song," said Brer Wolf, talking as sweet as molasses. "You catch on so quickly and harmonize so nicely, Brer Rabbit, that all you need to do is hum the song over after we get there."

"Surely, surely, I can do it," agreed Brer Rabbit as he strutted around.

On the night of the party, Brer Gilyard's house was full of creatures from everywhere. Brer Gilyard sat at the head of the long table, Brer Lion sat at the foot, and the four singers—Brer Wolf, Brer Fox, Brer Bear, and Brer Rabbit—sat together near the middle. All the little creatures, including Brer Rabbit, were so scared of Brer Gilyard that they hardly touched their food. But soon fiddlers began to play, and the party was on.

Brer Wolf leaned over and whispered to Brer Rabbit, "When we stand before the folks, don't get nervous. Act like the brave man you are. Just sing out your part loud and strong, because everybody likes to hear you sing. We'll support you."

160

"All right, Brer Wolf, but what am I supposed to sing?" asked Brer Rabbit.

"We'll sing a song that will make Brer Gilyard and all the creatures laugh. We'll pretend we're selling some sheep. Brer Fox, Brer Bear, and I will sing, 'Who sold Brer Gilyard's sheep?' And you'll answer with the chorus, 'Yes, yes, yes, I did.'"

"Oh, is that all?" replied Brer Rabbit. "I know I can sing that."

"I thought so, Brer Rabbit. That's why we're going to let you sing the second chorus all by yourself."

"Anything to amuse the folks, Brer Wolf," answered Brer Rabbit. "Let's get started."

So Brer Wolf sprang to his feet and asked Brer Gilyard to quiet down the creatures. He had something to say. Brer Gilyard clapped his hands, and everybody stopped eating and talking.

Brer Wolf bowed to the crowd and then spoke out, "Ladies and gentlemen, at this time I want to announce that four of the most popular singers in the Deep Woods will honor Brer Gilyard with a piece of music. The singers are Brer Bear, Brer Fox, myself, and that champion of all champion singers, Brer Rabbit!"

All the creatures clapped their hands and wings and made all sorts of noises. And Brer Rabbit put on his best airs after such a flattering introduction. "I'll show them a thing or two. I'll show them how to sing," he said to himself.

Then Brer Wolf hummed a time or two to get the quartet in tune. And then they began.

"Who sold Brer Gilyard's sheep?" they sang.

"Yes, yes, yes, I did," answered the chorus.

Everybody laughed. Then they sang again, only this time Brer Wolf, Brer Fox, and Brer Bear changed a word in the song.

"Who stole Brer Gilyard's sheep?" sang the three big creatures.

"Yes, yes, yes, I did," answered Brer Rabbit without thinking. And Brer Gilyard looked astonished.

But Brer Wolf went right on. "Let's sing this once more," he said. "The crowd is crazy about it."

"Who stole Brer Gilyard's sheep?" sang the three big creatures again.

"Yes, yes, yes, I did," responded Brer Rabbit again.

Then up jumped Brer Gilyard and grabbed poor old Brer Rabbit by the back of his neck! "I've a good mind to eat you right now, you good-for-nothing thieving varmint," roared Brer Gilyard.

"Oh, no, no! Don't eat him up now before your company," roared back Brer Lion. "Save him till morning and have rabbit hash for breakfast. Rabbit hash is good for breakfast."

"All right," agreed Brer Gilyard. "But I should eat that thieving creature, hide and all, for stealing my sheep. Especially since he bragged about it right to my face. Never mind—I'll save him until daylight and have rabbit hash for breakfast." So Brer Gilyard took Brer Rabbit outside and locked him up in his chicken coop for safe-keeping.

Pretty soon Brer Fox eased out of the house to see what

had happened to Brer Rabbit. Maybe Brer Gilyard had wrung his neck. But Brer Rabbit saw Brer Fox coming in the moonlight, and he raised an awful ruckus among the hens and roosters. This was too much for Brer Fox, who loved chickens. He crept up to the coop, while Brer Rabbit caught a fat hen by the neck and swung her around and around close to the chicken-house door. Brer Fox could see her and smell her.

"Hey there, Brer Rabbit. What're you doing in there, raising all that fuss with those chickens?" whispered Brer Fox.

"Why, man, I'm having the time of my life in here. These are the fattest hens I've ever seen in all my born days," boasted Brer Rabbit. "How come you don't come in here and help yourself? You like chicken."

"How do you get in?" asked Brer Fox.

"Just lift the latch and jump in," answered Brer Rabbit.

So Brer Fox lifted the latch and jumped in the chicken house. And as he jumped in, Brer Rabbit jumped out. Then Brer Rabbit slammed the door, shot the bolt, and said, "He, he, he, he, he! Brer Fox, Brer Gilyard's going to have fox hash for breakfast in the morning. I've got you this time. Good-bye—I'm gone." And down the road Brer Rabbit went, lickety-split, lickety-split.

Brer Wolf and Brer Fox Get a Big Surprise

WHEN BRER FOX DIDN'T COME BACK to Brer Gilyard's party, Brer Wolf slipped out of the house to look for him. He heard such a squawling and a cackling in the chicken house that he ran there first of all. And who did he see but Brer Fox a-raring and a-tearing around the coop, scattering feathers every whichaway.

"What on earth are you doing in there?" asked Brer Wolf. "Why isn't Brer Rabbit in there?"

"That rapscallion fooled me in here and latched the door," said Brer Fox. "Oh, if I could just get my teeth on him, I'd tear him to pieces."

"Yes, I'd do that, too. But first we'd better get out of here before Brer Gilyard eats us in place of Brer Rabbit in the morning," said Brer Wolf, unlatching the coop door. "Here, come on out. Let's go."

Brer Fox jumped out, and both creatures hotfooted it down the big road to a safe place.

"Phew, that was a close call," said Brer Fox when they stopped to rest.

"Yes, and now let's make a new plan to catch Brer

Rabbit," said Brer Wolf after he'd caught his breath.

"He's probably home in bed now," said Brer Fox. "The best thing to do is to hide and lay low in the morning, then catch him when he comes out to eat breakfast. He's bound to come out when he's hungry enough."

"All right," responded Brer Wolf. "We'll get a nap in the woods and set out for Brer Rabbit's house soon in the morning."

So they slept, but they were headed for Brer Rabbit's house long before daylight. They were determined to catch him this time.

But Brer Rabbit was a smart man. He was up and out of his house long before the varmints showed up. He figured that Brer Wolf and Brer Fox would try to catch him. So he decided to eat his peas and turnips early and get back home and stay indoors all day. But he tarried a minute too long on his last turnip. Brer Wolf saw his long ears poking up above a turnip top, and he moved to keep Brer Rabbit from running down the furrow to his house in the hollow gum tree, as he had planned.

"Come on, Brer Fox. I see him," whispered Brer Wolf. "Let's creep around to his house and cut him off. Keep your head low and crawl. He hasn't seen us yet."

So Brer Fox dropped low and crawled with Brer Wolf as quiet as two snakes, closer and closer to Brer Rabbit's house. Unaware of the two varmints, Brer Rabbit kept on chewing his last turnip, crunch, crunch, crunch. Then, crack! A stick popped under Brer Fox's foot. Zip, Brer Rabbit jumped two feet in the air, and like a streak of lightning he was off, lickety-split. But he was not headed

for home. Straight across the field he made tracks for a deep thicket.

Brer Rabbit ran like the wind and kicked up a dust across the field. But the big creatures gained on him. He cut across the field and made a circle for his house, but they crowded him closer and closer. He ran and he dodged and he dodged and he ran, but still they came closer and closer, and his house seemed far away. Brer Rabbit jumped over the bushes on the ditch bank. He flew through the bramble briars and the broom sage. Still Brer Wolf and Brer Fox gained on him every jump.

"They're too close for comfort," thought Brer Rabbit, as he spied his house in the gum tree. "But maybe I can make it."

Brer Rabbit gave one last big spurt across the yard, but Brer Wolf's hot breath was already on his heels. No, he couldn't make it. Time was too short. Brer Wolf's teeth were almost on him now. He'd grab him before he could slam the door. He was done for.

Then, zoom, zoom, zoom, zoom! Like bullets from a rifle, yellow balls of fire hit Brer Wolf and Brer Fox in the face and knocked them halfway across the yard. They rolled and tumbled and scratched and clawed. Everything went black.

"Balls of fire, what was that?" cried Brer Wolf.

"I'm shot, and burning all over," answered Brer Fox, still scratching.

"No, you're not shot. You've just been hit by my friends the hornets," said Brer Rabbit laughing, as he looked down from a knothole in the house. "And if you don't get up and skedaddle away from here this minute, I'll set my friends on you again. And this time they'll bung you up for sure."

Brer Fox and Brer Wolf jumped right up and ran out of Brer Rabbit's yard, bookety, bookety. And they steered clear of Brer Rabbit and his house for a long time after that.

Brer Rabbit Rescues His Children

BRER WOLF AND BRER FOX were still licking their hides days after the hornets had stung them in Brer Rabbit's yard.

"We'll get even with Brer Rabbit if it's the last thing we do," said Brer Wolf. "We'll play a trick on his children and lead them into Brer Gilyard's den. That'll pay back that pesky rascal for all he's done to us."

Now, Brer Rabbit had five children at home in the hollow gum tree. As long as they stayed inside or close to the house, nothing could hurt them. Whenever they went outside to eat turnip tops or drink spring water, Brer Rabbit would say, "You-all stay within hollering distance of the house, and don't you ever go near the big road. Brer Gilyard might get you."

Day after day Brer Wolf and Brer Fox spied on Brer Rabbit's farm, hiding in the bushes watching for Brer Rabbit's children. At last one day the five young ones strayed off to the big road. Brer Wolf and Brer Fox were ready. They had dressed up like women and had bonnets on their heads. And Brer Fox came down the road just a-playing on his guitar. Brer Wolf was by his side, and both were just a-dancing and a-singing:

"Well, Brer Rabbit skipped,
And Brer Rabbit hopped.
Brer Rabbit ate up the turnip top. . . ."

Brer Rabbit's children had never seen Brer Wolf and Brer Fox before. "Surely they must be good friends of our pappy," they said to one another. "They're singing his favorite song." So instead of running back home, the five children joined in the singing and the dancing, and down the big road they went, just a-waltzing and a-prancing to the sweet music of Brer Wolf and Brer Fox. And before they knew where they were, they came to a big cave at the side of the road.

"Let's play hide-and-go-seek," said Brer Fox. "You children go hide in the cave while Sis Wolf and I count up and play a tune. I'll count to twenty."

"But the cave is dark," said the children.

"The better to hide in," spoke up Brer Wolf.

So while Brer Fox played on the guitar and counted up to twenty, the children ran into the cave to play hide-and-go-seek. But Brer Fox and Brer Wolf knew this cave was the den of Brer Gilyard and Brer Lion, and when the children didn't come out again, the two tricksters were sure that Brer Gilyard had gobbled them up, so they went away and left them.

Now, Brer Rabbit missed his children. He called and he shouted their names all over the farm, but no answer came. He ran out to the big road and ran up and down and looked both ways. There was no sign of the children. Then he looked down at the sand and saw their tracks, along with those of Brer Wolf and Brer Fox. His heart beat fast. He followed the tracks. And the sand told him how the children had danced and pranced down the road right into the mouth of Brer Gilyard's cave. All the tracks went in, but none came out. Brer Gilyard had Brer Rabbit's children.

Now, maybe you know already that Brer Gilyard was a terrible dragon, as big as Brer Bear. His eyes were big like saucers, and his teeth were as long as pitchfork prongs. His nose was the size of a yardstick, and when he got mad, he breathed out fire and smoke. He was so ugly, he dared not travel in the daytime because all the little creatures ran from him. So he used Brer Lion in the daytime to fool the little creatures into his cave whenever they passed that way. He liked to eat these little folks, you know.

So Brer Rabbit stood before Brer Gilyard's cave wondering whether his children were living and how he might save them. At that time, Brer Lion walked out of the cave. Brer Rabbit moved back a pace or two.

"Howdy, Brer Rabbit. How are you today?" spoke up Brer Lion, wagging his tail all friendly-like.

"I'm feeling poorly, Brer Lion, poorly," answered Brer Rabbit.

"What's the matter?" inquired Brer Lion.

"I've lost my children," replied Brer Rabbit. "Have you seen them, Brer Lion?"

"Yes, I've seen them. They are in Brer Gilyard's cave. Don't you want to come in, too?" said Brer Lion, trying to tempt Brer Rabbit.

"No, sir, thank you," replied Brer Rabbit, still keeping his proper distance. "I won't go in this time. All those tracks are going in, and none are coming out." And Brer Rabbit left Brer Lion and went back down the big road.

Late into the night Brer Rabbit thought about his children in Brer Gilyard's den, and finally he got up and went back to the cave. Brer Rabbit crept up to the door. His heart was thumping. He poked his head inside and wiggled his whiskers. Nothing happened. Probably Brer Lion and Brer Gilyard were fast to sleep. At any rate, Brer Rabbit knew he had to go into that cave and see what had happened to his children.

So Brer Rabbit—he's smart, you know—he put his left hand against the side of the wall as he entered the pitch-black cave. That way, even though he couldn't see a thing, he figured he only had to turn around and put his right hand against the same wall to find his way out. So with one hand feeling the wall, he tiptoed deeper and deeper into Brer Gilyard's cave. The path turned and twisted like a long gourd vine. Deeper and deeper went Brer Rabbit, and scareder and scareder he became, looking for Brer Gilyard to jump out and grab him any minute.

At last, just as he was about to give up, Brer Rabbit saw a light ahead. He slowed down, and the light grew brighter. Then suddenly, right before Brer Rabbit's eyes, opened the biggest and brightest room he had ever seen in his whole life. Only the midday sun could shine like that. Brer Rabbit looked around. He saw no lamps, no candles anywhere. But from the ceiling and from the walls and from all around glittered a thousand diamonds, some as big as a guinea hen's egg. The room looked like a king's palace. In fact, in the center of the room stood a throne all covered with shining stones. On either side were great armchairs, big enough for a giant to sit in.

And on the throne slumped Brer Gilyard himself. He was sound to sleep and snoring like a bellows. To the right, with his head drooping, was Brer Lion; he was asleep, too. Brer Rabbit heard a squeaking sound. It came from way across the room. He looked up and saw a row of iron cages full of little creatures. And then he saw his five little children all in one cage. They were about to call him when he put one hand to his mouth as a sign for them not to speak. "Be quiet," he motioned with his lips. "I'll be back to get you out tomorrow night." The big creatures didn't hear him.

Before he left, Brer Rabbit counted ten cages in which he saw many of his old friends: Brer Turkey Gobbler, Brer Goosey Gander, Brer Rooster, Brer Possum, Brer Raccoon, and Brer Groundhog, all begging with their eyes for Brer Rabbit to please get them out. But Brer Rabbit was helpless. So he backed off into the dark tunnel once more, placed his right hand against the wall, and slowly crept out of the cave. Day was breaking when he reached the big road.

By the time Brer Rabbit arrived home, he had a plan all worked out in his mind. There was work to do. His first stop was Brer Spider's house. He knocked on the door, and Brer Spider opened it. Brer Rabbit sang:

> "Brother Spider, Brother Spider,
> Please weave me some thread
> To fetch back my children
> Before they're all dead. Umhum."

Brer Spider promised, then set to spinning a strong thread that no creature could see and no creature could break.

Then Brer Rabbit went to Brer Snake's house. And after getting him up, he begged:

> "Brother Rattler, Brother Rattler,
> Please give me some poison.
> Just put it in a bottle,
> And I'll use it with good reason. Umhum."

It took a while, but finally Brer Snake gave Brer Rabbit a little bottle of poison.

Then Brer Rabbit knocked on Brer Lightning Bug's door and sang:

> "Brother Bug, oh, Brother Bug,
> Won't you lend me some light
> That'll shine on my path
> In the dark of the night? Umhum."

Brer Lightning Bug wrapped up a spark of light in a green leaf and gave it to Brer Rabbit. "Thank you, sir," said Brer Rabbit.

And finally he found Brer Bear, at his meat market, and said:

> "Brother Bear, oh, Brother Bear,
> Please sell me a piece of meat
> To save my five children
> From a hungry man's teeth. Umhum."

Brer Bear cut off a piece of fresh mutton and put it in a bag. Then Brer Rabbit paid for the meat and took it home.

He didn't tarry very long, because pretty soon he slammed the door and hurried off to the Pee Dee River Swamp. Deep in the swamp Brer Rabbit found the longest fishing cane he could handle. He cut it down and dragged it to his house. Then he cut a long thorn from a locust tree and tied it to the tip of the fishing pole. After that, he had only to wait for the dark.

So Brer Rabbit waited for Brer Rooster to crow for midnight, and then he put the thread and the poison bottle in his pocket, fastened the light on his cap, threw the bag of meat over his shoulder, and started down the big road, dragging the fishing pole.

When Brer Rabbit reached the cave, his heart pounded with fear. He listened for any growling noises from inside. Then he fastened the thread to a bush, turned on the light in his cap, and quietly went into Brer Gilyard's cave, dragging the fishing cane behind him. He unwound the spider's thread as he moved along, deeper and deeper into the cave. When he reached the throne room, which shone as bright as day, he put away the thread and hid himself in a dark corner for a minute to get his bearings.

Then Brer Rabbit blinked his eyes and saw Brer Lion and Brer Gilyard lying out on the floor. They were snoring loudly. And bottles and bones were scattered all around. They must have had a party earlier that night, thought Brer Rabbit, and he looked with worry at his children and the little creatures still in the cages. Then Brer Rabbit poured the snake's poison on the meat and crept from his dark corner to one of the great chairs. He tossed the poisoned meat close to the mouths of Brer Lion and Brer Gilyard. Nothing happened. So he reached out with his fishing pole, and he jabbed Brer Lion in the ribs with the sharp thorn.

"Who's that biting me with his sharp teeth?" roared Brer Lion.

"Nobody," roared back Brer Gilyard. "You're dreaming. Go back to sleep."

All became quiet again. And then Brer Rabbit jabbed Brer Gilyard with the sharp thorn. Brer Gilyard sprang up and smacked Brer Lion with a blow. It would have killed a man.

"How come you bit me like that?" yelled Brer Gilyard, and fire shot out of his mouth.

Before Brer Lion could answer, they saw the fresh meat. Both grabbed for it.

"Umhum," roared Brer Gilyard. "You've been stealing my mutton."

"No, you've been stealing mine," growled Brer Lion. "And you tried to kill me while I was asleep."

Then both big varmints snatched the meat up in their mouths and began to pull and to tug. The fight was on. And Brer Rabbit jumped back to his dark corner and watched.

Brer Lion and Brer Gilyard, they pulled and they tore. They slapped and they scratched and they rolled on the floor. Scales and fur flew every whichaway. Chairs and tables were knocked over and about like matchsticks. Smoke and fire belched from Brer Gilyard's nostrils, while Brer Lion ripped open the dragon's side with his big claws. The little creatures screamed and hollered in their cages, and the cages shook as the big beasts fought, bellowed, and roared.

Then, just as Brer Rabbit thought that Brer Gilyard had killed Brer Lion, both of them began to wobble and to shake. Their eyes rolled from side to side, and both of them looked poorly and green around the gills. The poisoned meat was beginning to tell. And pretty soon Brer Lion and Brer Gilyard fell over and stretched out, stiff dead from the snake's poison. Brer Rabbit had won the battle for the freedom of his children and his friends.

When Brer Rabbit was sure the two varmints were stiff dead, he went to Brer Gilyard, took the keys from around his waist, and unlocked the doors of all the cages. Then he counted his children to make sure they were all there. And the other little creatures thanked Brer Rabbit for saving their lives.

176

"But how are we going to get out of here?" asked Brer Turkey Gobbler. "Nobody knows the way."

Brer Rabbit laughed and winked one eye. "Just one of you catch my hand, and the rest hold on to each other. I'll fetch you out in no time."

Then Brer Rabbit turned on the light in his cap, wound up Brer Spider's thread, and brought them all out to the big road just at daybreak. And from that day to this, there never was a lion or a gilyard in the woods of the Pee Dee River country to fool the little creatures into his cave, where all the tracks went in and none came out.

Who Got Brer Gilyard's Treasure?

THE DAY AFTER Brer Rabbit had brought the little creatures out of Brer Gilyard's cave, Brer Groundhog said, "We have nothing to eat and nowhere to live since we lost all we had while Brer Gilyard kept us in the cave as prisoners. What in the world are we going to do, Brer Rabbit?"

Brer Rabbit rocked back and forth in his chair on his piazza in front of the big gum tree, and he thought and he thought. "I've got it. I've got it, Brer Groundhog," he said at last. "We'll go down to Brer Gilyard's cave and bring out his gold and diamonds and give it to the poor creatures."

"You're like a rock in a weary land, Brer Rabbit, a shelter in a time of storm," shouted Brer Groundhog as he dashed off to tell his friends that the treasure would soon be theirs.

Before long, a big crowd came together in front of Brer Rabbit's piazza. He told them, "Tomorrow, my friends, we'll go together into Brer Gilyard's cave and fetch out the gold and the diamonds. Brer Mud Turtle, you be sure to bring along your sons with their strong backs to help tote the treasure out of the den. And everybody be at the mouth of the cave by sunup in the morning. Then by tomorrow evening, you'll all have enough to build your houses and buy all the vittles you need for a long time."

Brer Rabbit's good news spread through the Deep Woods like wildfire. When Brer Tiger and Brer Bear heard it, they immediately planned to take the treasure from Brer Rabbit and keep it for themselves. The fact is, they would have gone into the cave and brought out the riches if they had known how to get in and out without becoming lost. But Brer Rabbit was the only one who had that secret.

So Brer Tiger and Brer Bear set out for Brer Rabbit's house. They pretended to be friendly when they saw him, and they said, "Howdy, Brer Rabbit. You look especially fine today. You must be very happy."

"I am happy," said Brer Rabbit. "I've just found a way to help the poor creatures that Brer Gilyard and Brer Lion had mistreated so badly."

"Yes, we heard about that, Brer Rabbit," said Brer Tiger all innocent-like, "and we've come to talk to you about the treasure. Confidentially, we think you are making a big mistake to divide all that gold and diamonds among those poor creatures, when you might keep a part of it for yourself."

Brer Rabbit always said, "Trust no mistake, and jump from every bush that shakes." So he suspected that Brer Bear and Brer Tiger were up to no good. And he said to them, "My friends, I don't understand you. What do you mean about dividing the treasure? It doesn't belong to me. It belongs to the poor creatures that Brer Gilyard held in his cave so long."

"We mean, Brer Rabbit, that if you'll show us how to get in the cave and fetch out the treasure, we'll give you one part and we'll take the other two parts. How about it?"

Brer Bear frowned. "Speak up, man, speak up. We haven't got all day to stand here arguing with you."

Poor Brer Rabbit was in an awful fix now. He looked up and down the road for help, but no one was in sight, not even his friends the hornets. He was at the mercy of two dangerous creatures who could tear him to pieces with one blow of their paws. And he knew for certain that they would have eaten him, too, if they hadn't known he held the secret of how to get in and out of Brer Gilyard's cave. He was worth more to them live than dead.

"Never mind," threatened Brer Tiger. "If you don't show us how to get the gold, we're going to tie you up and choke you to death."

With that, they grabbed Brer Rabbit, dashed him to the floor, and tied him with a grass rope. Then they locked the door and took the key with them. And they said that if he didn't change his mind, they were coming back that night to eat him up. This looked like the end of poor Brer Rabbit.

But as soon as Brer Tiger and Brer Bear had left, one of Brer Rabbit's littlest friends, Brer Lizard, crept through a crack under the door, and he said to Brer Rabbit, "I heard everything that Brer Bear and Brer Tiger said to you, because I was hiding under the bannister rail. Now I want to help you."

"Oh, Brer Lizard, the Lord must have sent you. He's always on the side of right," said Brer Rabbit. "And you can help me. First, I want you to get word to all the creatures to be down in front of Brer Gilyard's cave the way I told them, first thing in the morning. Be sure to tell Brer Hooting Owl to be there, too, because we're going to need him to do the judging. Now, Brer Lizard, come a little closer. I want to tell you something secret and mighty particular." And then Brer Rabbit whispered in Brer Lizard's ear some secret plan that nobody could hear but the two of them.

When Brer Rabbit finished whispering, Brer Lizard crawled under the door again and ran off into the Deep Woods as fast as his legs could carry him. He hurried to all the friends' houses and told them how Brer Bear and Brer Tiger were going to kill Brer Rabbit because he refused to give the treasure to those two wicked creatures.

"All right, I'll be there," agreed Judge Hooting Owl when Brer Lizard told him how Brer Rabbit expected him to be at the cave in the morning. And he added, "I'll bring along my specs so I can see the treasure in the daytime."

It was nearly night now, and still Brer Lizard had to go and find Brer Ground Mole, Brer Groundhog, Brer Muskrat, and a whole passle of other creatures. And all the time Brer Rabbit was still lying on the floor, tied up with the big rope and locked in his house. Just before dark he heard the rumbling of Brer Bear's and Brer Tiger's feet as they mounted his steps. They unlocked the door and walked in.

"Well, Brer Rabbit, have you made up your mind to lead us through the cave in the morning to get the treasure? Or are you ready to die?" asked Brer Tiger.

And Brer Rabbit, not letting on about his plan, said, "A live rabbit is better than a dead lion, gentlemen. So I'm ready to take you to the cave in the morning. Now won't you untie me and let me stretch my legs?"

Brer Bear and Brer Tiger had nothing to fear since they were big and strong. So they untied Brer Rabbit. But they locked the door and kept the key. Then they went home, but they didn't go to sleep. And as soon as Brer Rooster crowed at sunup, Brer Bear and Brer Tiger unlocked Brer Rabbit's door and said, "Get up, Brer Rabbit. Let's get going."

So Brer Rabbit, Brer Tiger, and Brer Bear went to the cave, but everybody was there ahead of them. Brer Rooster, Brer Turkey Gobbler, Brer Goosey Gander, Brer Goat, Brer Deer, Brer Hooting Owl, Brer Mud Turtle and his sons, Sis Guinea Hen and her chickens, Brer Muskrat, Brer Ground Mole, and Brer Groundhog with all their families, and a whole crowd of other people were there. The sight of so many creatures surprised Brer Tiger and Brer Bear, but didn't surprise Brer Rabbit.

He went directly to the opening in the side of the hill that led to Brer Gilyard's den, but Brer Bear and Brer

Tiger kind of held back, as if they were afraid to steal the gold and the diamonds with so many homeless creatures looking on. They hadn't expected so many folks that soon in the morning.

"Come on, Brer Bear and Brer Tiger," called out Brer Rabbit. "We haven't got any time to lose. Let's get the treasure. Come on in the cave. See, I'm leading the way." And he skipped out in front of the two big creatures, as light as a feather.

But when Brer Bear and Brer Tiger followed him down the path toward the cave, the top of the ground suddenly sank beneath them. And before they knew it, both of them fell, kerplunk, right down into a deep, deep pit. There they were at the bottom of a trap that Brer Rabbit had ordered during the night. You see, that was the secret message he had asked Brer Lizard to give to the little creatures who live under the ground. The ground moles and the muskrats and the groundhogs had all pitched in together and had moved out the dirt in front of the cave, leaving only a thin crust on the top.

"Help, help," the two big creatures cried. "Get us out of here! Get us out of here!"

"Oh, no," said Brer Rabbit. "You stay down there. It's the best place for varmints like you. And now how about the treasure, my friends?" And Brer Rabbit showed all the little creatures where it was safe to walk, and they followed him into the pitch-black cave. Even old Brer Hooting Owl had to take off his specs to see in the dark. But after a while, the gold and the diamonds were

brought out, and then Judge Hooting Owl put on his
specs again and divided the treasure among all the little
creatures who deserved it.

After that, he spoke to the two big creatures down in
the trap. "Now, Brer Tiger and Brer Bear, you got
caught in the trap after trying to rob the poor creatures.
You deserve to be covered up with dirt and left to die.
But if you promise not to bother Brer Rabbit anymore,
and to let the creatures have the treasure that belongs to
them in the first place, we'll turn you loose and let you go
way back down in the Deep Woods."

"We promise, Judge Hooting Owl, never to bother Brer
Rabbit again. And we promise to let the other creatures
have the treasure," answered Brer Bear and Brer Tiger
together.

"Put down the ladder and let them climb out of the trap," ordered Brer Hooting Owl. "And don't you two try such a trick again as long as you live," he warned as the two big creatures slinked off out of sight, ashamed of themselves.

And that was the end of all the troubles that Brer Rabbit and his friends had with Brer Gilyard and the other bad creatures in the Pee Dee River Swamp. Once and for all Brer Rabbit had won out because he had *right* on his side!

Afterword

IN HIS LATER YEARS, Simon Brown became a devout Christian who faithfully prayed aloud every night before going to bed and every morning upon arising. One of my last recollections of my old friend and mentor is that of being awakened each morning by his melodious voice sending up praises to God.

Usually he began by thanking God for "sparing me one more time to see the light of another day." Then he prayed for forgiveness of his sins. "Lord, You know I'm as prone to sin as the sparks are to fly upward. But please, Sir, for Christ's sake, forgive me and save my poor soul from death and hellfire. And please, Sir, enable me to live right and do right this day."

Next Simon often asked God's blessings on members of his or my family, sometimes naming the one who needed help most. Occasionally his voice trailed off into a whisper, as if he were talking into God's ear in an agony of confidence or perhaps sharing quietly some great joy that was in his heart.

Invariably Simon closed his prayers something like

this: "Oh, Lord, I pray that my last days may be my best. And when I come to lay my head on my dying pillow, please, for Jesus' sake, take me in Your loving arms and carry me up to Glory. There I'll be free from all the troubles of this world, and I'll praise Your Holy Name forevermore. Amen and thank God."

My mother once asked Simon why he always said "Amen and thank God." He replied with a grin, "I reckon it's because I just feel I ought to thank Him for listening to a poor sinner like me."

That was Simon Brown.

I was away at school when Simon Brown died. He is buried in the "colored folks' cemetery" beyond the Bethesda Baptist Church in Society Hill.

I consider myself very lucky and very blessed to have known such a remarkable man—a philosopher, humorist, actor, and superb teller of tales. Simon Brown was the first man I ever heard who could "make the animals talk," and through this book I hope that neither he nor his tales will be forgotten.

About William J. Faulkner

"I collect stories the same way some people collect stamps. And the stories of my black ancestors have so much importance and so much beauty that I want to tell them to the world." So says William J. Faulkner, who, after having pursued other distinguished careers, has become a devoted folklorist.

Dr. Faulkner's first encounter with black folk literature came in 1900, when he was a boy of ten, and a gifted storyteller named Simon Brown was hired to work on his widowed mother's farm in Society Hill, South Carolina. Simon Brown had been a slave in Virginia, and he enthralled young William with his true tales of slave life and his imaginative tales of talking animals. In fact, Simon Brown's folktales so impressed the mind of young Faulkner that he has remembered all but a few and has faithfully recorded them in this book.

Although Dr. Faulkner is a talented storyteller himself, he claims he has never equaled the excellent voice and mannerisms of Simon Brown. Still, his children and grandchildren often asked him to "please tell us a story from the book that's inside you."

Other people of all ages also enjoyed hearing Dr. Faulkner tell the folktales of black Americans. Over the years, he has spoken to thousands of people at youth conferences of the Methodist Church, at college lectures for the American Friends Service Committee, and at countless gatherings of children in YMCAs, churches, and schools across the country.

In 1967, Dr. Faulkner was commissioned to lecture on Afro-American folk literature at schools throughout Dade County, Florida. For this work, he tape-recorded a number of Simon Brown's folktales, accompanied by brief talks about significant achievements by black people. The program was designed to improve the self-images of black students and to heighten the respect of white students for the black. The students responded enthusiastically, and this encouraged Dr. Faulkner to begin work on *The Days When the Animals Talked.*

Dr. Faulkner graduated from Springfield College, Springfield, Massachusetts, and received his doctorate in theology from the Chicago Theological Seminary of the University of Chicago. He worked several years as a YMCA secretary in Philadelphia, Atlanta, and Washington, D.C., and has been a pastor of churches in Atlanta and Chicago. For nineteen years, he served with distinction as University Minister and Dean of Men at Fisk University, in Nashville.

Now in his eighties, Dr. Faulkner is pursuing his latest career of folklorist in the hope that his work will help "to dignify the black storyteller and contribute to truer racial understanding."